2 batters

everyday chocolate cake

peanut butter-fudge polka dot cake

marshmallow-cocoa cake

chocolate-cherry cake

chocolate-peppermint cake

chocolate-sour cream batter

vanilla-sour cream batter

vanilla celebration cake

fun time surprise cake

crunchy, creamy coconut cake

strawberry and butterscotch whipped cream cake

cinnamon crumble cake

citrus-vanilla cream-glazed blueberry cake

1 magic mix

baking gold mix

bits of chocolate and sea salt cookies

pretzel-toffee-chocolate-cherry cookies

ginger-molasses cookies with orange zest

berry-cardamom cookies with toasted walnuts

fruit and nut brownies

malted milk-white chocolate brownies

chocolate-chocolate-chocolate cookies

peanut butter-chocolate cookies

double vanilla-spice brownies

caramelized milk brownies

peanut butter brownies

Baking Gold

Baking Gold

How to Bake (Almost) Everything with
3 Doughs, 2 Batters, and 1 Magic Mix

VANILLA

Jami Curl

**Photographs by Emily Kate Roemer
and Maggie Kirkland**

10

TEN SPEED PRESS
California | New York

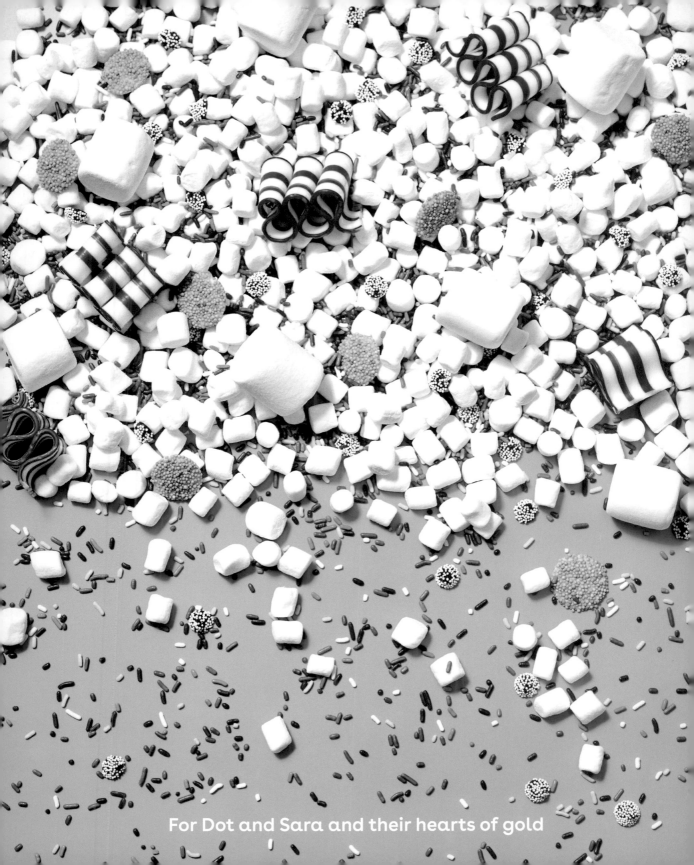

For Dot and Sara and their hearts of gold

contents

1   getting to gold

13   3 doughs

91   2 batters

143   1 magic mix

187   appendices

188   sharing gold
201   giving gold
205   materials and resources

209   acknowledgments

210   index

recipes and projects

Overnight Dough   16

Butter Dough   46

Brown Sugar-Oat Dough   74

Chocolate-Sour Cream Batter   96

Vanilla-Sour Cream Batter   118

Baking Gold Mix   146

buns and rolls

Caramel Sticky Buns   21

Gooey Cinnamon Swirls   25

Spiced Bubble Buns   29

Chocolate-Honey–Almond Butter Poufs   33

Brown Sugar–Cardamom Butter Stack-Ups   37

bars, tarts, and crisps

Coconut Jam Tarts   41

Jam Jambles   66

Sweet Cherry Crumble Bars   68

Maple-Pecan Not-Pie Bars   71

Blueberry-Coconut-Orange Ones   77

Goodie Snacktime Bars   78

Nutty Chocolate Oaties   80

Apple-Citrus Crisp   83

Apricot-Walnut Caramel Tarts with Honey Cream   87

cookies and brownies

Everyday Holiday Cookies   50

Citrus–Vanilla Cream Dots   55

Darling Buttercream Darlings   58

Sprinkle Pop Cookies   63

Nutty Chocolate Oaties   80

Bits of Chocolate and Sea Salt Cookies   149

Pretzel-Toffee-Chocolate-Cherry Cookies   153

Ginger-Molasses Cookies with Orange Zest   157

Berry-Cardamom Cookies with Toasted Walnuts   159

Peanut Butter–Chocolate Cookies   164

Chocolate-Chocolate-Chocolate Cookies   169

Malted Milk–White Chocolate Brownies   171

Fruit and Nut Brownies   173

Double Vanilla–Spice Brownies   177

Caramelized Milk Brownies   178

Peanut Butter Brownies   182

cakes

Everyday Chocolate Cake   99

Peanut Butter–Fudge Polka Dot Cake   103

Chocolate-Peppermint Cake   107

Chocolate-Cherry Cake   111

Marshmallow-Cocoa Cake   114

Vanilla Celebration Cake   123

Cinnamon Crumble Cake   126

Citrus–Vanilla Cream–Glazed Blueberry Cake   129

Fun Time Surprise Cake   132

Strawberry and Butterscotch Whipped Cream Cake   137

Crunchy, Creamy Coconut Cake   139

fillings, buttercreams, and more

Caramel-Pecan Sauce   21

Cinnamon-Sugar Dust   25

Bubble Bun Dust   29

Chocolate-Honey–Almond Butter   33

Cardamom-Ginger Butter   37

Vanilla Buttercream   50

Strawberry Compote   66

Sweet Cherry Compote   68

Maple-Pecan Filling   71

Blueberry-Coconut-Orange Topping   77

Apricot-Walnut Caramel   87

Honey Cream   87

Cream Cheese Buttercream   99

Peanut Butter Buttercream   103

Cocoa Fudge Sauce   103

Peppermint Buttercream   107

Cherry–Cream Cheese Buttercream   111

Marshmallow Glaze   114

Special Chocolate Buttercream   123

Citrus–Vanilla Cream Glaze   129

Butterscotch Whipped Cream   137

Caramelized Milk   178

baking gold reinventions

Coconut Sticky Buns   22

Chocolate Poufs   34

Cardamom-Raisin Stack-Ups   38

Cheese-and-Herb Stack-Ups   38

Apple, Butter, and Brown Sugar Tarts   45

Caramelized Milk and Coconut Tarts   45

Chocolate and Hazelnut Tarts   45

Nectarine and Blueberry Tarts   45

Raspberry Jam and Almond Tarts   45

Crispy Kale, Parmesan, and Egg Tarts   45

Goat Cheese and Pesto Tarts   45

Gruyère and Caramelized Onion Tarts   45

Aged Cheddar and Pear Tarts   45

Smoked Mozzarella and Tomato Tarts   45

Cut-Out Cookies with Buttercream and Sprinkles   52

Cinnamon-Sugar Darlings   60

Lemon Zest Darlings   60

Chocolate Buttercream Darlings   60

Candy Pop Cookies   64

Peanut Butter and Jam Jambles   67

Peanut Butter, Raisin, Cinnamon Goodie Snacktime Bars   79

Butterscotch, Cashew, Coconut Goodie Snacktime Bars   79

Chocolate, Peanut, Sea Salt Goodie Snacktime Bars   83

Apple-Vanilla Crisp   83

Spiced Apple Crisp   84

Apple-Cherry Crisp with Almonds   84

Peach-Blackberry Crisp   84

Cocoa Fudge–Glazed Peanut Butter Cake   104

Blueberry Crumble Cake with Citrus-Vanilla Cream Glaze   130

Blueberry-Orange Cake with Vanilla Bean Cream Cheese Buttercream   130

Peach and Butterscotch Whipped Cream Cake   138

Toffee Fudge Cake   139

Chocolate-Pecan-Toffee Cookies   151

Toffee-Chocolate Cookies   154

Peanut Butter Cookies   167

Chocolate-Chocolate–Peanut Butter Cookies   170

sharing gold

Best Brownie Party   190

Cookie Dough Drop-Off   195

Cookie Party   198

Sprinkle Party   200

Giving Gold   201

getting to gold

Here's the truth about me: I'm a hyper-focused, freakishly efficient, uncluttered, and orderly rule follower. I love tedious projects with lots of steps. I like pursuits that take a lot of time. I like neat and tidy, straight and organized, a place for everything and everything in its place. I tidy up my house upon waking, and tidying is the last thing I do before bed. I'm the kind of person who looks forward to cleaning day. I know. I sound like a lot of fun.

Here's another truth about me: I'm a recovering bakery owner. I took the same approach to my bakery as I do to life—it was focused, efficient, and orderly. Most recipes relied on elaborate multistep processes. Nothing came from a box or package. We made every component of every item we sold, from granola to jam, caramel to ice cream. If a recipe contained a nut, we candied it in sugar and spices first. Flour for cookies was loaded into a cold smoker and smoked over Oregon alder wood. Heirloom apples were sliced and allowed to rest, their resulting juice transformed into a caramel destined for the internal workings of an apple pie. White chocolate was caramelized, cooled, chopped, and mixed into cookie doughs. We dehydrated locally grown fruit and made mounds of marshmallows with honey and sea salt. We spent endless hours proofing brioche dough (made with fancy European butter) to poufy perfection.

These laborious processes were possible because I wasn't working alone. There was a talented team of professional bakers working with me to make them possible. We understood how to make the best use of time and how to accomplish tasks as efficiently as possible. We knew which components of a recipe to make ahead and what tools were the most useful for each job. Some of this was common commercial kitchen knowledge. Most of it was squeezed out of the hours we spent figuring out how to create authentic hand-made products that we could then produce day in and day out—starting at 3 am every morning.

Since my days as a bakery owner, the way I spend my time in the kitchen has changed. For example, I rarely have time for brioche—a pursuit I turned into a three-day process at the bakery. I've realized that a simple toasted nut tastes as good as a candied nut once it's buried in a cookie. I haven't caramelized white chocolate in ages. Instead, I've focused on creating bakery-worthy recipes that can be baked quickly and easily in my home kitchen. Pair this with an ability to organize and prepare like a pro baker (or an obsessive home-tidying control freak), and you've got what I've come to call Baking Gold—strategies and recipes that can do a lot with very little. Baking Gold features three doughs, two batters, and one baking mix that can be magicked into more than seventy-five unbeliev-able treats. With twenty-plus additional recipes for cookie fillings, cake toppings, and delightful mix-ins, you're looking at a jackpot of recipes.

I created Baking Gold for bakers like you. And bakers like me. We want recipes that eliminate unnecessary steps, follow streamlined processes, and are quick to come together without (ever!) relying on store-bought mixes or doughs. This cookbook is for bakers like us, and I can't wait to get started.

How Baking Gold Works

At home, I'm probably a lot like you. It's a bit of a scramble to find the time to bake. If I'm going to bake a chocolate cake or sprinkle-topped cookies or gooey sticky buns, they've got to be the best, and I've got to have a plan. And that plan has two parts: carefully chosen recipes and proven strategies for becoming a better baker. It all adds up to Baking Gold.

Part One: The Recipe

Choosing the right recipe to bake is an action that's as important as any step in the recipe itself.

Recipes should be trustworthy and not a waste of your time, ingredients, and effort. These are valuable resources! A recipe is even better when it makes the most of those resources by working in multiple ways.

Part Two: The Strategy

Over the years, I've collected a list of tips and tricks that I always use when I bake. I call them the Elements of Baking Gold. The elements are part of any baking plan I make, and they're the key to getting treats into the oven faster.

Element 1

Be prepared: The very first step of any recipe should be "read the recipe." I know this seems obvious—yet, here I am, reminding you to please start every recipe by reading the recipe. Once you've read the recipe, you'll have an idea of what comes first, what comes next, and how things end up. You can take a minute to grab the ingredients you need. You can visualize the steps you'll need to take to bake the treat you want to bake. And you'll have a solid understanding of the timing of a recipe. Make note of any resting or baking time, and use that time to tidy up, do dishes, or prep additional ingredients. Knowing what comes next and understanding the timing of a recipe is a very Baking Gold way to bake.

Element 2

Make notes: Whether scribbled in the margins of the cookbook or in a separate notebook, notes improve baking. I started making detailed baking notes one Christmas to remember how much cookie dough I needed to cover unexpected drop-ins, teachers' gifts, and Santa's cookie plate. After a few years of trying to remember what I had baked the previous year, I finally started making notes in the margins of my recipes about what I baked ("Christmas 2018: 4x dough plus 4x icing for cookies through Christmas Eve"). Notes enable you to foolproof your baking.

Element 3

Label smart: Always have a roll of tape and a permanent marker around because what you remember today you may not remember next week when looking in the freezer or pantry. Label everything—what's inside, the date it was opened, and the use-by date if it applies. And, please, label for baking: Label all frozen dough with date, dough type, oven temperature, bake time, and after-baking storage information. That way you won't even have to open a book when it's time to bake.

Element 4

Invest in two tools: Every baker should have a scale and a stand mixer.

A scale is the easiest and fastest way to better baking. Accurate measuring is essential, and the key to accurate measuring is a scale. I swear by scales. I live by scales. I love my scale. As for measuring cups and spoons? I do use them. I use them to scoop ingredients into bowls that are (you guessed it) on a scale. Switching to a scale doesn't mean you have to give up on your cutest spoons and measuring cups—they're always useful in your kitchen, even if they aren't exactly reliable tools for Baking Gold.

Get yourself a mixer: A stand mixer is the easiest and fastest way to prepare sugar and butter for the next steps of a cookie recipe and it will help Overnight Dough (page 16) come together fast. There are lots of ways to save on your first mixer, especially if you don't mind colors from last season. Major hint: Some manufacturers sell refurbished stand mixers for (way) less than half of the retail price (see Materials and Resources, page 208).

If you're interested in a third runner-up when it comes to trusty tools, get yourself an oven thermometer so you always know the true temperature inside that oven of yours.

Element 5

Learn to love parchment: I love parchment paper about as much as I dislike nonstick cooking spray (and I really dislike cooking spray). Cooking spray builds up over time and develops a strange residue that is almost impossible to remove from baking pans. Save money, time, and your sanity by switching to parchment paper sheets (see Materials and Resources, page 206). I buy a box of one thousand 24 by 16-inch sheets at my local food-service supply store (you don't need a membership to shop there). Then I cut the sheets in half to create 12 by 16-inch sheets so I can quickly and easily line sheet pans and 9 by 13-inch pans. I also cut the sheets into 6 by 8-inch pieces for lining the cups of standard muffin pans (instead of buying cupcake liners). You'll find a million uses for parchment paper (one of my favorites is for wrapping up edible gifts), and it will never leave behind a funky, sticky mess on your favorite pans.

How to line 9 by 13-inch pans with parchment paper: Place the paper over the 9 by 13-inch pan and center it. In a single movement, press the parchment down into the pan, using your hands to smooth it out to the edges of the pan and up the sides. The paper will have creases at the edges and corners, and once you fill it with batter or dough, it will stay in place. Once baking is finished and your cake, brownies, or bars have cooled, you can use the sides of the parchment to lift the treat out of the pan. Very easy.

Element 6

Create space: Dedicate a spot in your kitchen for baking tools, equipment, and ingredients. Buy ingredients in bulk and store them in easy-to-open containers. Label everything. The point is to cut out all the time you'd normally spend looking around for a pan or a spatula or a spreader or an ingredient. Because it's all in one spot (and organized and labeled), you'll save time searching. That time can be spent on an even better endeavor—baking! An efficient and time-saving baking pantry means better baking.

Element 7

Use what you have: If a recipe calls for dark brown sugar and you only have light brown sugar, what do you do? For any recipe in *Baking Gold*, you should use the brown sugar you have! The difference in flavor between the two sugars won't have a big effect on your cookies or brownies. The same rule applies to chocolate: If you have semisweet and the recipe calls for dark, don't let that keep you from baking. Milkier chocolate will be creamier and sweeter, darker chocolate will be more bitter. If you have salted butter in your fridge and the recipe calls for unsalted, not to worry. Simply adjust the amount of salt you use in the recipe, keeping in mind that a stick of salted butter contains approximately 1 gram of salt. Vanilla extract can be Madagascar, Mexican, or even vanilla bean paste. Using the brown sugar, chocolate, butter, and vanilla you have (rather than waiting to go shopping) means you can start baking now.

Element 8

Prepare more than you need: It's a fact that if you have ingredients ready for baking, you'll bake more often. If you're toasting nuts or chopping chocolate, toast or chop more than you need the day you are baking. Keep toasted nuts in your freezer. Chopped chocolate in your pantry means an even faster finish. Frozen fruit is always handy, and jars of fruit compote in your fridge will never go to waste. A container of Baking Gold Mix (page 146) in the pantry is the fastest way to quick cookies and brownies.

Element 9

Embrace instant baking: When my freezer is stocked with frozen cookie dough and other treats, I feel ready to take on any treat emergency. Whether I need cookies for a meeting tomorrow or kids find their way to my house after school, I'm ready. Cookies can be on your plate in mere minutes if you mix, scoop, and freeze the dough ahead. When I'm mixing cookies, I like to freeze some of the dough from the batch I'm making. That way we always have cookie dough ready for the oven. When I make tarts with Overnight Dough (page 16), I try to do the same thing: save some of the dough for the freezer. I half-bake the tart shells and freeze them. When I'm short on time, I grab them from the freezer, top them, and get them into the oven.

Element 10

Believe in reinvention: Baking Gold wouldn't be as gold if it weren't for the art of variation. Nearly every recipe in the *Baking Gold* collection can become an entirely new sweet with a few swapped ingredients. This reinvention of a recipe is one of my favorite moments in baking: When I've made a cookie or a bar I know I love (and I know others love), I dream up another way to use it, flavor it, or bake it. See page vii for a complete list of Baking Gold Reinventions.

Element 11

Find your perfect size: If you want your brownies or bars cut into perfect squares, by all means, grab a ruler and do that. If you'd rather cut some big pieces and some small pieces, do that. Diamonds or rectangles instead of squares? Go ahead and get fancy—you made these treats, you can cut them any way you'd like. Don't get tripped up trying to get things exact and even all the time. I want to make cutting a pan of brownies the least of your worries.

Element 12

Believe in scoops: I'm talking about commercial portioning scoops—not mere ice cream scoops—that can handle every scoopable baked treat from tiny cookies to jumbo muffins. Scoops make fast work of shaping cookie dough and result in uniform baking. For the cookies in this book, I like to use a 2 Tbsp / 30ml scoop. (For more on scooping technique, see page 154.)

Element 13

Reduce and reuse pans: I've found that reducing the number of baking pans I own has streamlined my baking process. I only use three types of pans to create all of the recipes in this book. Why? Because it's easier, more efficient, and saves space. The three pans are: Sheet pans, muffin pans, and 9 by 13-inch pans.

I use 18 by 13-inch sheet pans with low sides, often referred to as a half-sheet trays or half-sheet pans, for cookies, tarts, and toasting nuts and coconut.

Standard (not mini) 12-cup muffin pans are used for some of the buns and tarts made with Overnight Dough (page 16) and Brown Sugar–Oat Dough (page 74).

For cakes, bars, and brownies, I use 9 by 13-inch metal (not nonstick) baking pans that are light in color and have sharp corners and straight sides. These sides produce even baking and a consistent rise.

Chocolates, Fruits, Nuts, and Sugars

If you love making recipes your own by switching up ingredients, then the Baking Gold way of baking is perfect for you. Start with the recipes as they're written, then venture out beyond what's on the page, calling on different ingredients to reinvent the recipes. A good place to start? Right here, with chocolates, fruits, nuts, and sugars. These ingredients are easy to swap and substitute, making the recipes of *Baking Gold* a little more your own.

Chocolates

The chocolates of Baking Gold are milk and semisweet and dark, white and creamy, chips or chopped. And don't forget about cocoa powder! The recipes calling for cocoa powder will work with whatever cocoa powder you have around—natural or Dutch process.

Fruits and Nuts

Baking Gold is all about choice. There's a ton of choice when it comes to the fruits and nuts that you can add to cookies, brownies, bars, and other treats. Most any nut and dried fruit will work in these recipes. You can pick from cashews, apricots, cherries, cranberries, hazelnuts, walnuts, almonds, or any of your favorites.

Sugars

The sugars of Baking Gold come in all shapes and sizes—granulated sugar is pure cane sugar and is used almost everywhere in the book. Brown sugar can be dark or light. Pearl sugar adds a sweet, delightful crunch. And sprinkles! Oh, the sprinkles.

dutch process cocoa powder

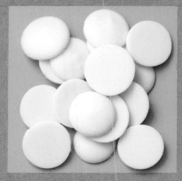

white chocolate wafers

semisweet chocolate chips

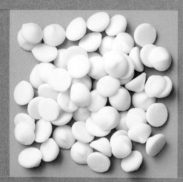

white chocolate chips

choppec dark chocolate

mini chocolate chips

dark chocolate wafers

natural cocoa powcer

chopped white chocolate

cashews

slivered almonds

dried
blueberries

walnuts

dried cranberries

hazelnuts

dried cherries

sweetened shredded coconut

salted
peanuts

pecans

dried apricots

powdered sugar

granulated sugar

white nonpareils

crystal sugar

white jimmies

pearl sugar

light brown sugar

3 Doughs

My vision for better baking is built on simple recipes that can do a lot. And these doughs can do exactly that.

Overnight Dough is about to become your new favorite. It's a pillowy-soft yeast dough, and it's not difficult or scary—it practically makes itself overnight. I love Overnight Dough dressed up as gooey cinnamon rolls and simplified as buttery dinner rolls.

Overnight Dough starts by simply mixing the ingredients. Then it rests in the refrigerator overnight. The refrigerated dough is then rolled and shaped according to the recipe you're using. It's at this point that the dough can either be left to rest in a warm spot or it can go back in the fridge to rest overnight (again!). The next morning, when you want sticky buns fresh from the oven, all you have to do is let the dough rise in a warm spot, bake, and enjoy.

I've made Butter Dough at least a thousand times. It's magical because it can work for nearly anything you can imagine—cookies, tarts, and bars. It's buttery, a touch flaky, and entirely enjoy-able (if I do say so myself). What makes this recipe Baking Gold? The fact that it can be pressed, rolled, sliced, cut out, or shaped into almost any treat you can imagine. It lasts forever when frozen. (I've made extra dough at Christmas and cut it into heart shapes and frozen them so I have a stockpile of ready-to-bake cookies come Valentine's Day.)

Brown Sugar–Oat Dough is a kitchen treasure. It's buttery and oaty and ideal for topping an apple crisp. It can be pressed into a pan and used as a tart base. It can even be transformed into granola bars (that taste a thousand times better than the store-bought ones). I suggest you try it out in the Apple-Citrus Crisp (page 83) as soon as you can. What makes this dough pure Baking Gold? Its supreme versatility.

overnight dough
in five
simple steps

1 mix → 2 overnight rest in refrigerator

3 shape

4 proof in warm spot

5 bake

or

1 mix → 2 overnight rest in refrigerator

3 shape

4 hold in refrigerator overnight

5 proof in warm spot

6 bake

overnight dough

This dough is such a surprise. By all accounts, it shouldn't be as fantastic as it is—it makes fluffy rolls and buns, it's full of flavor, and it's endlessly useful. All of that and it's also incredibly easy to make. It doesn't add up, does it? Once this dough is mixed it needs an overnight rest in the refrigerator (where it gets its name). After that overnight rest it's ready to use.

solid gold

Overnight Dough uses instant yeast. I don't mean active dry yeast; I mean instant yeast and, yes, there's a difference: Instant yeast needs no blooming (that step when you mix the yeast with a little warm water and a bit of sugar to activate it). Instant yeast can be added with the flour, no blooming required. As for warm water, there's no need to fuss with a thermometer here. Instead, use water that is not hot to the touch yet still feels warm. You want it warm enough for handwashing—not cold and not steaming hot.

Combine the butter, sugar, and salt in the bowl of a stand mixer fitted with the paddle attachment. With the mixer on medium speed, cream the ingredients until light and fluffy, approximately 3 minutes.

In a medium bowl, stir together the flour and yeast.

Add 1 cup / 120g of the flour-yeast combination, plus the water, to the mixer bowl. Mix until smooth (this will take about 2 minutes), then add the remaining 2 cups / 240g flour-yeast combination and the egg.

Run the mixer until the flour is incorporated, then stop the mixer and scrape the sides and bottom of the bowl. Now mix for 5–7 minutes on medium speed. The dough will start to look like it's forming a thick web that is pulling away from the sides of the bowl and still sticking to the paddle attachment.

½ cup / 113g unsalted butter, at room temperature

½ cup / 100g granulated sugar

1 tsp / 5g kosher salt

3 cups / 360g all-purpose flour

1 packet / 2¼ tsp / 7g instant yeast

¾ cup / 175g warm water

1 large egg, beaten

Yield: Approximately 3 cups / 780g dough

continued →

overnight dough, continued

Scrape the dough out of the mixer bowl and into a bowl or container with a lid. Cover and let the dough rest at room temperature for 20–30 minutes before refrigerating overnight.

After an overnight rest (or two nights if that works better for you), your dough is ready to use in the following recipes.

Double the Dough

Double every ingredient in the recipe, including the yeast. Your mix time (after all the ingredients have been added to the mixer) will be about 3 minutes longer (about 8 minutes total). You'll have about 6 cups / 1.5kg dough.

Easy Proofer

If your oven is new, it might have a proof setting. If not, you can get creative. Turn on the oven, let it heat up (if you have other baking to do, the temperature you need to use for that is fine), and clear a space in the cabinet, right next to the oven, that is large enough for your proofing pan. Once the oven has heated, and you can feel its warmth radiating into the cabinet next door, put the pan of buns or rolls in the cabinet. Close the door to keep in the heat: instant proofer. This works with the Bake setting on toaster ovens, too. And if you don't have space in the cabinet adjacent to your oven, you can still make use of its heat: Heat the oven, set a towel on your stovetop, and put the pan of whatever you're proofing on top.

caramel sticky buns

My favorite part of making these buns is spooning the sauce over them after they're arranged on a platter. They are a stunning sight to see. The sauce is shiny and the buns take on an almost shellacked look. Delight sets in once you realize they're as soft as air, with a touch of sticky from that sauce. I love to make these buns on slow weekends when we don't have to rush to be anywhere or do anything. Sitting around the table with sweets and coffee and buzzy conversation—it's my favorite place to be.

solid gold

Caramel Sticky Buns are studded with toasted pecan pieces. To toast your nuts, preheat the oven to 350°F. Line a sheet pan with parchment paper and arrange the nuts in a single layer. Toast for approximately 5 minutes, then remove the pan from the oven and give it a little shake. Put the pan back in the oven and toast for 2 to 3 minutes more, taking care that the nuts don't develop any dark spots. The pecans are ready to use, or let them cool, then store them in an airtight container.

You'll need two unlined standard 12-well muffin pans for these buns. An unlined pan makes it easier to scoop the sauce out of the wells and onto the buns.

Make the Caramel-Pecan Sauce: Combine the brown sugar, maple syrup, corn syrup, butter, cream, salt, and vanilla in a medium saucepan over medium heat. Once the butter starts to melt, occasionally stir the contents of the pan and allow them to come to a boil. Boil briefly—about 10 seconds—then remove the pan from the heat. Stir in the pecans. The sauce is ready to use immediately, or you can transfer it to a jar or other container. Let the sauce cool completely, uncovered. Once cooled, the sauce will be very firm. Rewarm it slightly to make it easier to spoon it into the muffin pan. The jar of sauce can be covered and stored in the refrigerator for up to 1 month.

continued →

Caramel-Pecan Sauce

1½ cups / 325g brown sugar

¼ cup / 75g maple syrup

¼ cup / 75g light corn syrup

½ cup / 113g unsalted butter

¼ cup / 60g heavy cream

1 tsp / 5g kosher salt

1 Tbsp / 18g pure vanilla extract

1½ cups / 150g pecan pieces, toasted

1 recipe Overnight Dough (page 16)

Yield: 16 buns

caramel sticky buns, continued

Scoop 2 spoonfuls of the sauce into the bottom of 8 wells of each muffin pan.

Next, shape the dough into 16 balls that are about 3 Tbsp / 48g each, by rolling the dough on a flour-coated work surface with your palm. Roll until the dough forms a tight ball, then place the dough on the sauce in the well—there's no need to press down on them.

Proof the buns in a warm spot (about 80°F) until they have doubled in size, approximately 90 minutes.

Preheat the oven to 350°F.

Place each pan on a sheet pan (to catch the bubbling caramel) and slide them into the oven. Bake for 15–18 minutes, until the buns are golden brown. A little overbaking is better than a little underbaking.

Let the buns cool in the pans for about 5 minutes, then lift them out of the pans and arrange on a serving platter. Spoon the syrup that's left in the wells over the buns, coaxing the pecans out of the baking pans, too.

Leftover buns can be stored, well wrapped, at room temperature for up to 2 days. Day-old buns can be warmed in a microwave or 350°F oven.

Baking Gold Reinvention

Coconut Sticky Buns

Replace the pecans with toasted sweetened, shredded coconut. To toast coconut: Spread it in a single layer on a parchment-lined sheet pan. Bake at 350°F for 10–15 minutes, until the coconut is a mix of pale golden brown to medium golden brown. Stir and then set aside to cool.

Make the sauce as directed, replacing the pecans with 1½ cups / 130g toasted coconut. You can always make the sauce with a mix of coconut and pecans, adjusting amounts of each to your liking.

gooey cinnamon swirls

These cinnamon swirls are buttery, extra-cinnamony, and soft in the middle—in other words, these are my dream cinnamon rolls. And talk about easy! These can be prepped a day ahead and refrigerated in the baking pan. That way you simply have to let them rise and then bake the morning you want to enjoy them. As for leftovers, they'll be great warmed up on the second day, and if they make it to the third day, they'll still be worth eating. On the fourth day, if you're crazy enough to still have them around, you should most definitely enjoy them again.

solid gold

I love the process of making cinnamon rolls because I adore the motion of spreading soft butter on dough. After the dough is gilded with butter, it gets a storm of cinnamon and sugar poured on top. It's the combination of the sugar melting with the butter that gives these swirls their signature gooey nature. And yes, as you're cutting the rolls and moving them to the pan, the cinnamon sugar will shower out of the cut pieces. Don't leave it behind! Scrape up all that dust (as directed in the recipe) and sprinkle it on top of the rolls once they're in the pan—this move is key to these gooey gems.

Make the Cinnamon-Sugar Dust: Place the sugars and cinnamon in a small bowl and whisk to combine. Set aside until ready to use.

Line a 9 by 13-inch pan with parchment paper (see Element 5, page 4).

Sprinkle flour over your work area. Scrape the dough from the bowl you refrigerated it in right into the center of that flour. Use your hands to pat the dough into a rough rectangle—this step helps the dough turn into an actual rectangle once you get going with a rolling pin. Grab a rolling pin and roll the dough into an approximate 12 by 15-inch rectangle. Now use a butter knife to spread the softened butter over the dough, making sure

continued →

Cinnamon-Sugar Dust

1 cup / 200g granulated sugar

3 Tbsp / 40g brown sugar

2 Tbsp / 12g ground cinnamon

1 recipe Overnight Dough (page 16)

¾ cup / 170g unsalted butter, at room temperature and very spreadable

Yield: 16 swirls

gooey cinnamon swirls, continued

to spread it all the way to the edges. Sprinkle the sugar mixture over the butter, covering the dough all the way to the edges.

Now you're ready to roll the dough into a cylinder. Start with a short side of the dough and use a bowl scraper or spatula to push the dough into the beginning of a roll. Dust the dough with a little flour right where it meets your work surface, and then, if it's helpful, continue to use the scraper or spatula to roll it onto itself to make a tight, even cylinder.

Now you're ready to cut the cylinder into rolls. Cut it into 16 equal pieces—if you're a fan of precision, a ruler will help here. Use a knife to cut a roll from the dough, then immediately place it into the parchment-lined pan.

You'll trail some cinnamon sugar along the way, and that's fine—we'll get to that in a minute. Once all the rolls are in the pan you'll have four rows of four, with space between each row. Your work surface will be covered with Cinnamon-Sugar Dust. Scrape it all up and shower it over the rolls in the pan (this will give them a crunchy-sugary-cinnamony finish that you'll love).

Proof the swirls in a warm spot (about 80°F) until they have doubled in size, approximately 90 minutes.

Preheat the oven to 350°F.

Slide the pan into the oven and bake for 35–40 minutes. The rolls should be a deep golden color. If they're not, add a few minutes to the baking time. The rolls will have puffed up and baked together beautifully.

Allow the rolls to cool in the pan for about 10 minutes (or less time if you can't stand waiting). You can remove the rolls from the pan one at a time or use the parchment paper to lift them from the pan, transferring them to a platter for serving.

Leftover rolls can be stored, well wrapped, at room temperature for up to 4 days. Day-old rolls can be warmed in a microwave or 350°F oven.

Choosing Cinnamon

For baking, I prefer a strong, spicy cinnamon that I can really taste in my treats. I keep Vietnamese cinnamon in my pantry and reach for it more often than not when baking. It has a higher oil content than standard cinnamon and disperses nicely throughout baked goods (see Materials and Resources, page 206).

spiced bubble buns

If there's a secret ingredient to these buns, it's the nutmeg included in the Bubble Bun Dust—the sugary stuff the buns get dipped in before baking. Nutmeg adds a nutty depth to the dust, and the Bubble Buns won't be the same if you leave it out. Speaking of Bubble Bun Dust, I have a feeling you're going to wonder where it's been all your life. It's great in coffee, on buttered toast, and in fruit crisps and cobblers.

solid gold

Bubble Buns are made up of tiny balls of dough that are tightly rolled and then dipped in butter and Bubble Bun Dust (of course). The rolling of all those tiny balls may seem daunting, so now's the time to recruit a helper. With two people rolling, you'll cut your prep time down. And if there's no one around to help? Try rolling the dough with both your right and left hands simultaneously. The art of the double roll takes some practice. Once you get it, you'll be making Bubble Buns in half the time, even without a helper.

Make the Bubble Bun Dust: Place the sugar, cinnamon, salt, and nutmeg in a small mixing bowl and whisk to combine well. Set aside until ready to use.

Line a standard 12-cup muffin pan with 6 by 8-inch parchment paper squares (see Element 5, page 4).

Working with approximately 2 tsp / 10g dough at a time, roll the dough on a lightly floured surface with a cupped hand until you have a round, compact little "bubble" of dough. Dip the bubble into the melted butter and then roll it in the Bubble Bun Dust. As you roll and dip and dust, nestle six bubbles into each well of the muffin pan. Start with three on the bottom and stack the remaining three on top like a pyramid (you can't mess up this arrangement, I promise, so get the dough balls in there and don't worry too much about it). Repeat the rolling and the arranging of six bubbles of dough in each well of the muffin pan until you've got twelve buns of six bubbles each.

Bubble Bun Dust

1 cup / 200g granulated sugar

1 Tbsp / 6g ground cinnamon

Rounded ¼ tsp / 2g kosher salt

½ tsp / 1g ground nutmeg

1 recipe Overnight Dough (page 16)

1 cup / 226g unsalted butter, melted

Yield: 12 buns

continued →

spiced bubble buns, continued

Proof the buns in a warm spot (about 80°F) until they have doubled in size, approximately 90 minutes. The buns will puff up and look very doughy.

Preheat the oven to 350°F.

Bake for 25–28 minutes, until you can see that the buns are golden brown underneath that dusting of cinnamony sugar. Let the buns cool for 5–10 minutes. Use the parchment to lift the buns from the pan. Leave the parchment paper in place—it will hold the buns together while they cool and make handling easy.

Bubble Buns are terrific straight from the oven. Leftover buns can be stored, well wrapped, at room temperature for up to 2 days. Day-old buns can be warmed in a microwave or 350°F oven.

chocolate-honey-almond butter poufs

Oh, these poufs are special. Everything about them, from their filling to their shape, makes them unlike any bakery treat you've had before. There's no need for individual shaping of buns here—the dough gets rolled out, the filling gets spread on, and the whole thing is baked together to golden greatness. I like to sprinkle crystal sugar or pearl sugar on the poufs after they've been brushed with an egg wash. The sugar adds a crunchy texture to the buns that drives me wild. For tips on finding crystal sugar and pearl sugar, see Materials and Resources (pages 205–206).

solid gold

Once you get the technique down for shaping and filling this dough, you'll quickly see that you can do a ton with it. The possibilities for fillings are beyond imagination. You can switch out the almond butter for any other nut butter, or use your favorite chocolate-hazelnut spread. And don't forget about the savory possibilities; cheese, herbs, and sauces will work too. If you go savory, replace the sprinkle of sugar over the egg wash with sea salt flakes.

Make the Chocolate-Honey–Almond Butter: Begin by melting the chocolate in a double boiler or a heatproof bowl set over (but not touching) a pan of simmering water. When half of the chocolate is melted, remove the double boiler from the heat and stir until the remaining chocolate has melted. Set aside to cool for 10 minutes.

In a medium bowl, stir together the almond butter, honey, salt, and vanilla. After the chocolate has cooled, pour it into the bowl with the almond butter mixture and mix well until combined.

It's best to use the butter immediately (while it's still spreadable). Of course, you can use it once it has cooled; you'll simply need to rewarm it in a small saucepan over low heat or in the microwave until it's spreadable. The butter can be stored in a lidded jar at room temperature for up to 1 week.

Chocolate-Honey-Almond Butter

12 oz / 340g chocolate, chopped (2 cups)

1¼ cups / 12 oz / 340g crunchy almond butter

¼ cup / 85g honey

1 tsp / 5g kosher salt

2 tsp / 12g pure vanilla extract

1 recipe Overnight Dough (page 16)

1 large egg

1 tsp / 5g water

Pearl sugar or crystal sugar

Yield: 8 poufs

continued →

chocolate-honey-almond butter poufs, continued

Dust your work surface generously with flour. Plop the dough into the center of the flour and roll it into a vertical rectangle that is 10 by 16 inches, with the long side closest to you. Use additional flour to unstick any sticky spots.

Spread the nut butter over the bottom 5 inches of the dough, then fold the dough over and press the edges together to seal. You now have a piece of dough filled with chocolate that is 5 × 16 inches.

Use a bench scraper or a spatula to help lift the dough free from your work surface, using more flour to unstick it as necessary. Transfer the dough to a piece of parchment paper by sliding the paper under the dough as you lift it up. Move the parchment paper to a sheet pan.

Use a knife to gently cut the dough into eight pieces that are each 2 inches wide. Do not separate the pieces—simply make the cut marks while keeping the pieces together.

Proof the poufs in a warm spot (about 80°F) until they have doubled in size, approximately 90 minutes.

Preheat the oven to 350°F.

Use a fork to mix the egg with the water. Use a pastry brush to gently apply the egg wash to the dough tops and sides, taking care to not miss any spots or to tear or deflate the dough. Sprinkle the sugar over the dough.

Bake for 30–40 minutes, until golden brown.

Let the poufs cool for 20–30 minutes before cutting them apart along the cut-lines. You can cut the larger pieces in half crosswise to make 16 servings.

Leftover poufs can be stored, well wrapped, at room temperature for up to 2 days.

Baking Gold Reinvention

Chocolate Poufs

For plain chocolate poufs, substitute up to 2 cups / 300 to 340g chopped chocolate for the nut butter filling. Cut, proof, egg wash, and bake as directed.

brown sugar-cardamom butter stack-ups

Is it fair to have a favorite? Because, from start to finish, these multilayer buttery, spicy puffy treats are my favorite to make and eat. I love the process of making these—making the dough, mixing the fragrant butter, cutting and stacking and layering and baking. Oh my, it's almost too much! Then they go into the oven and come out as buttery layers of brown sugar spice dough that are baked to crunchy-edged perfection. You're going to love them.

solid gold

Perhaps the highlight of this recipe is the compound butter—a mix of butter, brown sugar, and spices. Mixing these together to form a sweetened and flavored butter means the stack-ups are easier (and less messy) to make. The sugar and spice can't fall off the dough if they're mixed into the butter! Also, skip typical muffin pan liners and put that parchment to work. Cut parchment into 6 by 8-inch pieces. Place the stack-ups in the center of each piece of parchment. Fold up the edges of the parchment to cup the stack-ups and then nestle them in the wells of the pan. Once baked, the pieces of parchment create little serving cups.

Make the Cardamom-Ginger Butter: Place the butter, brown sugar, cardamom, ginger, vanilla seeds (if using), salt, and pepper in the bowl of a stand mixer fitted with the paddle attachment. Mix on medium speed until the butter comes together and turns creamy, about 3 minutes. The butter is ready to be used or can be wrapped and stored in the refrigerator for up to 1 week. The cardamom butter is easiest to use when it's at a very spreadable room temperature. If you've stored the butter in the refrigerator, remove it and allow it to sit at room temperature for at least 2 hours before using.

Sprinkle flour over your work area. Scrape the dough from the bowl right into the center of that flour. Use your hands to pat the dough into a rough rectangle—this step helps the dough turn into an actual rectangle once you get going with a rolling pin. Grab a rolling pin and roll the dough into an approximate 12 by 18-inch rectangle. Use additional flour to unstick any

Cardamom-Ginger Butter

¾ cup / 170g unsalted butter, at room temperature

1 cup / 215g brown sugar

1½ tsp / 3g ground cardamom

1 tsp / 2g ground ginger

1 vanilla bean pod, split and seeds scraped out (optional)

½ tsp / 3g kosher salt

¼ tsp / 1g freshly ground black pepper

1 recipe Overnight Dough (page 16), cold

Yield: 12 stack-ups

continued →

sticky spots. Spread the Cardamom-Ginger Butter evenly over the entire surface of the dough, taking care to not snag the dough and tear holes in it.

Cut the dough into 2-inch squares. You can do this by scoring the dough at 2-inch intervals across and down, then cutting the dough on those score marks to create 2-inch squares. If scoring the dough is too tedious for you, you can also simply cut the dough into 2-inch squares (that's what I do). You'll end up with 54 in total. Once cut, gather 4 squares and stack them on top of each other. Nestle the stack, cut sides up, into the center of a piece of cut parchment. Place this bundle into the well of the muffin pan. Repeat until you've used all the squares and have 12 stack-ups ready to go. You'll have a few squares of dough left over—I pick the nicest squares when making my stacks, then I discard the scrappier pieces.

Proof the stack-ups in a warm spot (about 80°F) until they have doubled in size, approximately 90 minutes.

Preheat the oven to 350°F.

Bake the stack-ups for 25–27 minutes. They'll be beautifully puffy, golden brown, and bubbling with butter and sugar. Cool in the pan for 5 minutes. Use the parchment paper to lift them from the pan. Leave the parchment paper in place—it will hold the stack-ups together while they cool and make handling easy.

These spiced, buttery layered buns are sigh-inducing when warm from the oven. Leftover buns can be stored, well wrapped, at room temperature for up to 3 days. Day-old buns can be warmed in a microwave or 350°F oven.

Baking Gold Reinventions

Cardamom-Raisin Stack-Ups

After you've smothered the dough in the spicy butter, sprinkle on ½ cup / 75g raisins (golden or regular) and press them into the dough a bit. Cut, stack, and bake as directed.

Cheese-and-Herb Stack-Ups

Roll the dough, brush with up to ¼ cup / 50g olive oil, and sprinkle with 1 tsp / 8g sea salt. Top with 1 to 1½ cups / 100 to 150g grated cheese (any cheese works) and dried herbs (such as basil or oregano). Press the cheese into the dough. Cut, stack, and bake as directed.

coconut jam tarts

Coconut Jam Tarts are extremely simple—almost too simple. The first trick is to use high-quality apricot preserves. The coconut adds a special spark because its texture is softy and chewy yet toasty and crunchy. And you don't have to stop at apricot and coconut for your tarts. Get creative! You can go from sweet to savory and back again. You can bake tarts that have all the same toppings or mix it up and go with eight different versions.

solid gold

Making Coconut Jam Tarts teaches you to shape, proof, egg wash, and half-bake the tart dough—all the steps you need to know to turn the dough into any tart you desire. For a freezer stash of ready-to-bake tart dough, make a double recipe of Overnight Dough (see page 18 for tips on doubling) and freeze the half-baked tart shells. Later, you can pull the half-baked shells out of the freezer, decorate them with the toppings of your choice, bake at 350°F (don't thaw first) for 20–25 minutes (depending on the topping), and have fresh-baked tarts in about 30 minutes. (See Element 9, page 5, for more on "instant" baking.)

Line two sheet pans with parchment paper. Sprinkle flour over your work surface.

Divide the dough into eight equal pieces weighing about 3 oz / 95g each. Roll one piece into a 6- to 7-inch circle. Fold the edges of the dough onto itself to create a cute little folded border—the dough won't build up or hold its shape like a true crust (the crimped edge is more of a finishing touch). Repeat until you've shaped all of the dough, dusting your surface with a little more flour to prevent sticking. Place the shaped dough on the prepared pans (four per pan).

Proof the dough in a warm spot (about 80°F) until puffy, about 45 minutes.

Preheat the oven to 350°F.

1 recipe Overnight Dough (page 16)

1 large egg

1 tsp / 5g water

1 cup / 340g apricot preserves

1 cup / 85g sweetened, shredded coconut

Yield: 8 tarts

continued →

coconut jam tarts, continued

Make an egg wash by cracking the egg into a small bowl, adding water, and mixing with a fork until it's a uniform eggy color with no streaks of yolk visible.

Use a pastry brush to apply the egg wash to each tart shell, covering the dough all the way to the edges. The shell should glisten uniformly with the egg wash.

Half-bake the shells for 8–10 minutes, until they turn a pale golden color. (To freeze the shells, cool completely, then wrap tightly, label, and freeze.)

Top each shell with a few spoonfuls of apricot preserves and a good sprinkling of coconut, breaking apart the flakes as you sprinkle it on (the coconut tends to stick).

Slide the pans into the oven and bake for 15–20 additional minutes, until the tarts are golden and puffy and the coconut is toasted in spots.

The tarts can be served warm from the oven or at room temperature. Store any leftover tarts, well wrapped, at room temperature for up to 3 days.

continued →

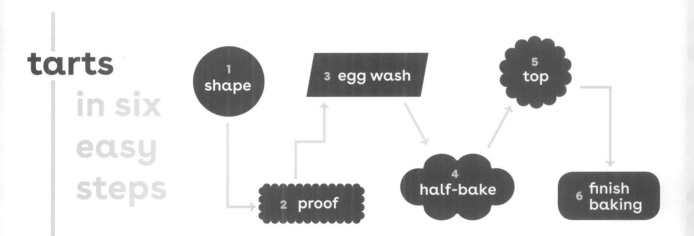

tarts
in six
easy
steps

1 shape
2 proof
3 egg wash
4 half-bake
5 top
6 finish baking

raspberry jam
and almond

goat cheese
and pesto

nectarine and
blueberry

apple, butter, and
brown sugar

crispy kale,
parmesan, and egg

chocolate and
hazelnut

Apple, Butter, and Brown Sugar

Toss apple slices in brown sugar and cinnamon. Arrange the slices on half-baked tart shells. Dot the tops with butter. Bake at 350°F until the apples soften and the tarts are golden, 15–20 minutes.

Caramelized Milk and Coconut

Top half-baked tart shells with Caramelized Milk (page 178) and sweetened, shredded coconut. Bake at 350°F until the coconut is toasty in spots, 12–15 minutes.

Chocolate and Hazelnut

Top half-baked tart shells with chopped chocolate or chocolate chips and chopped hazelnuts. Bake at 350°F until the chocolate melts, 8–10 minutes.

Nectarine and Blueberry

Sliced nectarines and peaches are both perfect for this tart, and you can use fresh or frozen fruit. If using frozen, simply toss the nectarine or peach slices with the blueberries and a little granulated sugar. Add a splash of vanilla extract and arrange the fruit on half-baked tart shells. Bake at 350°F until the fruit is soft and bubbly, 20–25 minutes.

Raspberry Jam and Almond

Spread 2 spoonfuls of jam on each half-baked tart shell. Top with slivered almonds. Bake at 350°F until the tarts are golden, 15–20 minutes.

Crispy Kale, Parmesan, and Egg

Place chopped kale in a bowl. Drizzle with olive oil and sprinkle in salt, black pepper, and lots of grated Parmesan. Arrange the seasoned kale in a nest on each half-baked tart shell. Crack an egg into a small bowl and slide it out of the bowl into the kale nest. Repeat for the remaining tarts. Bake at 350°F until the egg white turns white and the yolk is set to your liking.

Goat Cheese and Pesto

Smooth 2 spoonfuls of basil pesto on each half-baked tart shell. Top with crumbled goat cheese. Bake at 350°F until the tarts are golden, about 10 minutes.

Gruyère and Caramelized Onion

Shred or thinly slice Gruyère cheese. Top each half-baked tart shell with the cheese. Nestle a tangle of caramelized onion on top of the cheese. Bake at 350°F until the cheese is melted and the tarts are golden, about 12 minutes.

Aged Cheddar and Pear

Shred or thinly slice aged Cheddar cheese, arranging it on the half-baked tart shells. Top the cheese with thinly sliced pear. Bake at 350°F until the pears are soft, the cheese is melted, and the tart is golden, 15–20 minutes.

Smoked Mozzarella and Tomato

Top half-baked tart shells with shredded or thinly sliced smoked mozzarella cheese. Bake at 350°F until the cheese is warm and melty. Thinly slice tomatoes. Top the tarts with 1–2 slices of tomato, a pinch of sea salt flakes, and black pepper.

butter dough

Butter Dough is an indispensable pastry kitchen miracle. I've been making it for as long as I can remember, and I've used it for about everything I can think of—from cookies to tart dough. It's buttery, uncomplicated to make, and over-the-top versatile. Whether it's smeared with buttercream (see page 50) or the base of Maple-Pecan Not-Pie Bars (page 71), it is Baking Gold.

solid gold

The fastest way to get this dough ready for baking is by making it with a stand mixer. It'll take about a hundred times longer to make this by hand. (Slight exaggeration? Possibly. Still, trust me. See Element 4, page 4, and save time by giving this a whirl in your magic mixing machine!)

The dough can be made ahead and refrigerated for up to a week. Frozen, whether pre-shaped into cookies or pressed into a 9 by 13-inch pan, the dough can keep for 3 months or more (and you can bake from frozen without thawing). Remember, if you've got salted butter and nothing else in your fridge, you can still make this dough—use the salted butter, and eliminate the salt called for in the recipe. (See Element 7, page 5, for more about working with what you have on hand.)

1½ cups / 339g unsalted butter

1 cup / 200g granulated sugar

3 large egg yolks

1 Tbsp / 18g pure vanilla extract

3¾ cups / 453g all-purpose flour

1 tsp / 5g kosher salt

Yield: Approximately 5 cups / 1.04kg dough

Place the butter in the bowl of a stand mixer fitted with the paddle attachment. Turn the mixer to medium speed and beat for 5–7 minutes, until the butter is nice and shiny. Scrape the sides and the bottom of the bowl. Add the sugar and mix on medium for 4–5 minutes, until the butter and sugar become fluffy and light. Scrape the sides and bottom of the bowl again.

With the mixer on low, add the egg yolks one at a time, mixing between each addition and adding the vanilla with the third yolk. Mix until the eggs are fully incorporated. Scrape the sides and bottom of the bowl.

Place the flour and salt in a separate bowl and whisk to combine. Slowly add the flour mixture to the mixer bowl and mix on low until a dough forms and the flour is no longer visible.

continued →

butter dough, continued

After mixing I like to prepare the dough for how it will be used. Bars, pressed cookies, sliced cookies, and cut-out cookies all have different needs, and preparing the dough for that now will save you tons of time later. Once the dough is mixed, follow the instructions for bars, pressed or scooped cookies, sliced cookies, or cut-out cookies.

For bars: Line a 9 by 13-inch pan with parchment paper (see Element 5, page 4). Following the recipe of your choice, press the Butter Dough evenly into the bottom of the pan, making sure to fill the corners of the pan. The dough is ready to use now, or the pan can be wrapped and refrigerated or frozen until you're ready for it.

For pressed or scooped cookies: Scoop the Butter Dough out of the mixer bowl and onto a piece of parchment paper. Flatten the dough with your hands to make a 6 by 9-inch rectangle. (This will make the dough easier to portion for cookies— it's tricky to work with a boulder of cold dough.) Wrap the rectangle and refrigerate until firm.

For sliced cookies: Divide the batch of Butter Dough in half. Plop one half of the dough into the middle of a piece of parchment and shape the dough into a rough cylinder. Fold the parchment over the dough so the dough is in the center. Press the flat edge of a bench scraper into the dough where it meets your work surface—this will form a crease. Press the bench scraper into the crease while pulling the bottom half of the paper in the opposite direction that you're pressing the bench scraper. While pulling on the bottom half of the paper, move the bench scraper along the crease so that the pressure on the dough is somewhat even. As you press and pull, the paper will tighten around the dough, creating a nice, tight cylinder. Repeat for the other half of the dough. Ideally you will have created two 6-inch-long cylinders of dough that are tightly formed with no pockets or holes throughout the cylinder. These cylinders will be sliced into ¼-inch-thick cookies, 24 cookies per cylinder.

Refrigerate the dough until firm enough to slice by wrapping that same parchment around the cylinder and twisting the ends closed. To help the dough hold its shape in the refrigerator, cut open a paper towel tube (lengthwise), nestle the cylinder of dough inside, and use a piece of tape to secure the roll.

For cut-out cookies: Place the Butter Dough on a piece of parchment paper. Place another piece of parchment on top and flatten (or roll) the dough until about 1 inch thick. Refrigerate until firm.

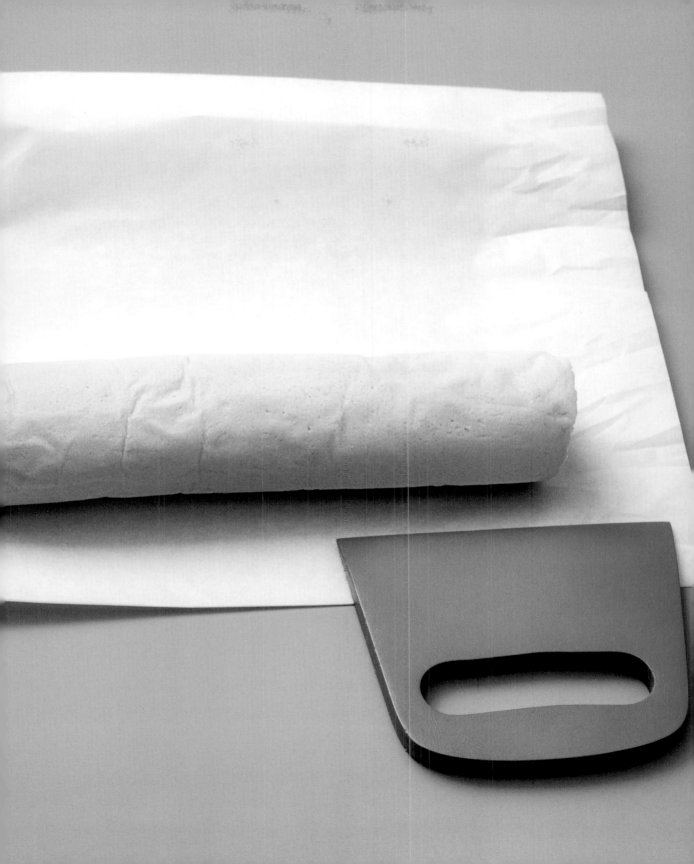

everyday holiday cookies

Thanks to the extraordinary usefulness of Butter Dough, it's my pleasure to let you in on a little secret. Cookies with icing and sprinkles no longer need to be reserved for holidays, thanks to these Everyday Holiday Cookies. They're easy enough that you don't need to wait for the magic of the Christmas season to bake them. Now Groundhog Day, movie nights, and even regular Wednesday afternoons can be holiday cookie occasions. All you have to do is roll the dough into a cylinder (see page 48) then slice, bake, and decorate.

solid gold

Cookies made with Butter Dough should be baked when the dough is very cold (frozen is preferred). This is true for any cookie that you want to hold its shape while baking. Round cookies, star cookies, flamingo cookies, unicorn cookies—every shape of cookie made with Butter Dough will bake more consistently and with nicer edges if the dough is very cold when it goes into the oven. How cold? If the dough isn't frozen, it should be refrigerated until it's extra-firm. What's extra-firm? If you press the dough with your fingertip, it will hold its shape instead of yielding to the pressure.

Preheat the oven to 350°F. Line two sheet pans with parchment paper.

Slice the frozen cylinder of dough into ¼-inch-thick rounds. Transfer the cookies to the prepared sheet pans, placing them about 1 inch apart. Bake for 10–12 minutes, until you see the edges of the cookies start to take on a golden hue. Let the cookies cool to room temperature on the sheet pans.

Make the buttercream: Place the butter in the bowl of a stand mixer fitted with the paddle attachment. Beat the butter on medium speed until smooth, 3–5 minutes. Scrape the bowl, then add the powdered sugar and vanilla. Mix on low. With the mixer running, add the milk, a little at a time. The sugar

- 1 recipe Butter Dough (page 46), shaped into a cylinder, frozen

Vanilla Buttercream

1 cup / 226g unsalted butter, at room temperature

11 cups / 1.25kg powdered sugar, sifted

1 Tbsp / 18g pure vanilla extract

½ cup / 113g whole milk

Sprinkles in custom colors (see page 200)

Yield: Approximately 48 cookies

continued →

will reduce in volume and the contents of the mixer will start to look like buttercream. Keep mixing until the buttercream is smooth and spreadable and not at all runny. The buttercream is ready to use. You can keep the buttercream, stored airtight at room temperature, for up to 2 days. For longer storage, refrigerate airtight for up to 1 week. To use buttercream that has been refrigerated, remove it from the refrigerator, leave it covered, and let it come to room temperature. Give the buttercream a good stir with a sturdy spoon before using.

Now you're ready to decorate the cookies. Pour the sprinkles into a shallow bowl. Using either a butter knife or a mini offset spatula, spread a nice layer of buttercream on a cookie. Dip the cookie, buttercream-side down, in the sprinkles and give it a gentle press so the sprinkles stick. It's best to decorate one cookie at a time because the buttercream tends to dry quickly (and it's difficult to get sprinkles to stick to dry buttercream). Another decorating option for these cookies is to simply sprinkle the sprinkles onto the buttercream (rather than pressing on a layer).

Let the decorated cookies sit for about 1 hour, until the buttercream is completely set. The cookies can be gently stacked in an airtight container and stored at room temperature for up to 5 days.

Baking Gold Reinvention

Cut-Out Cookies with Buttercream and Sprinkles

Roll the dough until it's even and ¼ inch thick. Refrigerate the dough until it's firm to the touch (it will make for easier cutting). Use your favorite cookie cutters to cut the dough into shapes. Freeze the cut cookies until they're very firm, at least 30 minutes or up to overnight. Bake in a 350°F oven for 10–12 minutes for medium cookies (15–18 minutes for larger shapes), until you see the edges of the cookies starting to turn golden. And if you love colored buttercream, now's the time to add a few drops of gel coloring to a bowl of buttercream (I love pastel buttercream on a cookie!). Top with buttercream and sprinkles.

citrus-vanilla cream dots

Here you have a cookie that is cute and simple—a delightful dot of creamy vanilla and bright citrus. A snap to make (even though they seem extra fancy), spoonfuls of dough are pressed flat then baked, then the tops are glazed with Citrus-Vanilla Cream Glaze. Fancy! And easy.

solid gold

Of course, this style of cookie is endlessly expandable. Think about it: A cookie like this can be topped with almost anything. Cocoa Fudge Sauce (page 103) and a cherry. Chocolate-Honey–Almond Butter (page 33), or even Marshmallow Glaze (page 114). You could even double them up to make sandwich cookies. Simply top a cookie with a spoonful or two (your preference) of a filling such as warm Chocolate-Honey–Almond Butter and press another cookie on top. The sandwich cookies will keep for 2–3 days in an airtight container at room temperature.

1 recipe Butter Dough (page 46)

Granulated sugar for dipping

1 recipe Citrus–Vanilla Cream Glaze (page 129)

Yield: Approximately 48 cookies

Preheat the oven to 350°F. Line two sheet pans with parchment paper.

Using a flat-bottomed glass or mug, press about 1 tablespoon of dough into a flat round that is about ¼ inch thick. If the cookie sticks to the glass, use a butter knife to ease it off. Dip the bottom of the glass in a bit of granulated sugar and repeat to form the rest of the cookies. Transfer the cookies to the prepared pans, placing them approximately 1 inch apart. Bake for 10–12 minutes, until you see the edges of the cookies starting to turn golden. Let the cookies cool to room temperature on the pans.

When the cookies are cool, place a spoonful of glaze in the center of a cookie and use the back of a spoon to smooth it out, right to the edges. (I love it when the glaze comes over the edge of the cookie slightly.) Repeat for the rest of the cookies. Set aside until the glaze has set, 20–30 minutes.

The cookies will keep for 2–3 days in an airtight container at room temperature.

darling buttercream darlings

Oh, these cookies! They are literally darling. I wrap them up as presents and pile them on plates for parties. They're an adorable addition to any holiday cookie collection, especially when the edges are rolled in festive sprinkles. I can never decide between Vanilla Buttercream and Peppermint Buttercream for these beauties. For that reason, I've included both here.

solid gold

While it's acceptable (and recommended!) to make Butter Dough simply so you can make these cookies, you can also use any leftover dough to make as many or as few of these darlings as you'd like. The dough can be refrigerated for more than a week or frozen for months and the buttercream filling can be, too. Once you mix the dough, it's easy to roll it into little balls and line them up on a sheet pan to slide into the freezer (you don't even have to cover it). When the dough balls are frozen solid—in about 30 minutes—you can place them all in a resealable bag for easy freezer storage. When it comes time to bake, simply slice the balls in half and bake—you don't even have to thaw them.

Divide the dough into rounded tablespoons (about 20g dough per cookie). Place the dough between your palms, rolling it until it forms a tight ball. It takes only a few seconds to shape each ball. Repeat the rolling until you've used all of the dough. Transfer the balls to a sheet pan and freeze until very firm, about 30 minutes.

When you're ready to bake, preheat the oven to 350°F. Line two sheet pans with parchment paper.

Place the sugar in a small bowl. Slice each ball of dough in half and toss in the sugar. Place the cookies on the prepared pans cut-side down. Bake for 15 minutes, or until golden around the edges. Let the cookies cool on the pans.

1 recipe Butter Dough (page 46), chilled for 15 minutes, or until somewhat firm

1 cup / 200g granulated sugar

1 recipe Vanilla Buttercream (page 50) or Peppermint Buttercream (page 107)

Sprinkles in custom colors (page 200)

Yield: Approximately 48 darlings

continued →

darling buttercream darlings, continued

Once the cookies are cool, top half of the cookies with a ¼-inch-thick layer of buttercream. Press another cookie onto the buttercream to create a darling little ball-shaped cookie. You'll have a little buttercream oozing out between the cookies. Roll that edge in the sprinkles for the cutest finish. Repeat for the rest of the cookies.

The cookies can be stored in your cookie jar (or other storage container) at room temperature for 3–5 days.

Baking Gold Reinventions

Cinnamon-Sugar Darlings

After you cut the balls of dough in half, roll each half in Cinnamon-Sugar Dust (page 25) and bake as directed. Fill the cookies with Vanilla Buttercream.

Lemon Zest Darlings

Transform Butter Dough into Lemon Butter Dough by adding the zest of a large lemon to the butter in the recipe, creaming them together, and then proceeding as directed for the Butter Dough. Use the dough to make Darling Buttercream Darlings, filling the cookies with Vanilla Buttercream.

Chocolate Buttercream Darlings

Bake the Darlings as directed and fill with Special Chocolate Buttercream (page 123) or Chocolate-Honey–Almond Butter (page 33).

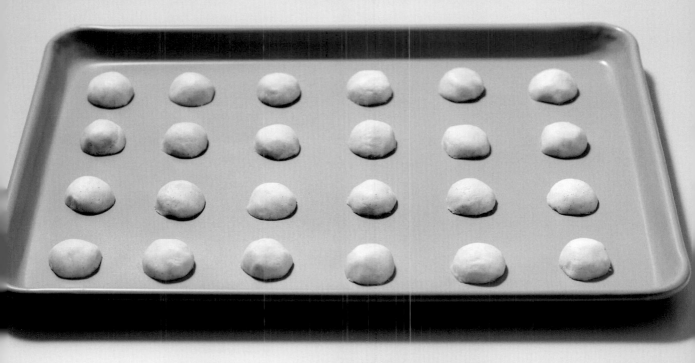

sprinkle pop cookies

Bright, speckled rainbow sprinkle cookies are the happiest cookies I know. I happen to think that rainbow sprinkles are completely perfect for these cookies. If you disagree, use whatever color of sprinkles you prefer. Another idea for these cookies? Ice cream sandwiches. Freeze the baked cookies until they are frozen, then add a layer of ice cream to the bottom of one cookie and top with another.

solid gold

Don't skimp on the time these cookies spend in the freezer or refrigerator prior to baking. Cold dough bakes into better cookies that hold their shape in the heat of the oven. If you do re-roll and re-cut dough scraps, be sure to chill the dough again before baking.

1 recipe Butter Dough (page 46), mixed just until the flour is no longer visible

1 cup / 170g rainbow sprinkles

Yield: 36 cookies

Add the sprinkles to the dough. Mix on medium until the sprinkles are evenly distributed throughout the dough.

Lightly dust your work surface with flour. Scoop the dough from the mixer bowl onto the work surface. Press the dough into a flat rectangle, wrap in plastic, and chill until it's firm enough to roll.

Preheat the oven to 350°F. Line two sheet pans with parchment paper.

Roll the cold dough to ¼ inch thick. Cut out cookies, using cutters of your choice. Transfer the cookies to the prepared sheet pans. Freeze until firm, about 20 minutes.

Bake the cookies for 10–12 minutes, until the edges are golden.

Let the cookies cool to room temperature on the pans. The cookies can be stored in your cookie jar (or other storage container) at room temperature for 3 days.

continued →

sprinkle pop cookies, continued

Baking Gold Reinvention

Candy Pop Cookies

Crushed candy takes these cookies to new heights—peppermint candy (especially at Christmas), fruity candy, butterscotch, and even sour candy are fun to try. Substitute 1 cup / 185g smashed hard candy for the sprinkles. While the cookies are baking, you may notice that the edges are starting to weep a bit of melted candy. This is perfectly normal. Immediately after baking, grab a butter knife and reshape the cookies in the spots that need it. The candy is sticky and the cookies will stay put.

jam jambles

Fun for everything from lunch box sweets to a picnic dessert, these jam-filled bars are easy to make and even easier to customize with the fruit compote of your choice. Strawberry is my favorite, yet blackberry or raspberry would be a wise choice for a jammy Jamble. (Pictured on page 76.)

solid gold

Now seems like a smart time to mention that, generally speaking, unparalleled baked goods are the result of quality ingredients, including fruit, butter, chocolate, nuts, and any other bits and pieces that go into making Baking Gold recipes worth eating. For Jam Jambles you'll want to use excellent strawberries, fresh or frozen (I prefer to use frozen because they don't require hulling and are usually picked and frozen at their peak). Quality goods make quality goods.

Make the compote: Combine the strawberries and vinegar in a saucepan and cook over medium-low heat until the fruit is soft and has released some juice. Add the sugar 1 cup / 200g at a time, stirring between additions until the sugar disappears. Increase the heat to medium and bring the fruit and sugar to a boil. Boil for 12–15 minutes, stirring occasionally. Turn off the heat and let the compote cool before using. The compote can be spooned into a jar and refrigerated for up to 1 month.

Preheat the oven to 350°F. Line a 9 by 13-inch pan with parchment paper (see Element 5, page 4).

Press 3 cups / 600g of the dough into the bottom of the pan. Refrigerate the pan until the dough is firm to the touch, about 20 minutes. Refrigerate the remaining 1½ cups / 300g dough until you're ready to top the Jambles with it.

Slide the pan into the oven and bake for 20–25 minutes, until the edges of the dough are golden. The base is now ready for the compote.

Strawberry Compote

4 cups / 600g frozen strawberries

2 Tbsp / 30g apple cider vinegar

4 cups / 800g granulated sugar

4½ cups / 900g Butter Dough (page 46)

Yield: 12 large or 24 small bars

Spread about 2 cups / 650g compote evenly over the top of the baked base, leaving a ¼- to ½-inch border around the perimeter. Using the coarse side of a cheese grater, grate the remaining cold dough over the jam. Slide the pan back into the oven and bake for 30–40 minutes, until the grated dough is golden in spots.

Let the bars cool completely, then use the parchment to help lift them from the pan. Cut into bars (see Element 11, page 7) and serve. The bars can be stored in an airtight container and refrigerated for up to 3 days.

Baking Gold Reinvention

Peanut Butter and Jam Jambles

Warm ½ cup / 135g crunchy peanut butter until it's spreadable. Before adding the strawberry compote, spoon the peanut butter over the dough. Top with the compote and then swirl them together over the dough, leaving a ¼- to ½-inch border around the perimeter. Top with the grated dough and bake as directed.

sweet cherry crumble bars

Buttery dough meets sweet cherries in this deep, dark, and luscious bar. While I like to eat these cold (straight from the fridge), they're also dreamy when slightly warm and served with a spoonful of lightly sweetened whipped cream. That said, I have been known to soften vanilla bean ice cream, mash up these bars, mix them in, and freeze the whole thing. Then I serve big scoops of Sweet Cherry Crumble Bar ice cream and everyone is happy.

solid gold

Sweet cherries are introduced to Butter Dough by way of a compote that's made with dark sweet cherries from (gasp!) a can. My favorite canned cherries are from Oregon Specialty Fruit and are available online and in grocery stores (see Materials and Resources, page 205). Double the recipe for the compote and you'll have some to stow in your refrigerator to use later (see Element 8, page 5). The Chocolate-Cherry Cake (page 111) is a fantastic use for cherry compote.

Make the compote: In a medium saucepan over medium heat, combine the cherries and syrup of 1 can with only the fruit from the second can. Stir in the salt and cinnamon. Bring to a simmer and cook for 25–30 minutes, stirring occasionally. The compote will have reduced and thickened. Remove the pan from the heat and stir in the almond extract. Use immediately or let the compote cool, then cover and refrigerate for up to 1 week.

Preheat the oven to 350°F. Line a 9 by 13-inch pan with parchment paper (see Element 5, page 4).

Press 2½ cups / 500g of the dough into the bottom of the prepared pan. Refrigerate the pan until the dough is firm to the touch, about 20 minutes. Slide the pan into the oven and bake for 20–25 minutes, until the edges of the dough are golden. Remove the pan from the oven and set it aside until you're ready to add the compote and topping.

Sweet Cherry Compote

2 (15 oz / 425g) cans Dark Sweet Cherries, pitted in syrup

½ tsp / 3g kosher salt

½ tsp / 1g ground cinnamon (see page 26)

½ tsp / 2g almond extract

4 cups / 800g Butter Dough (page 46)

½ cup / 60g slivered almonds, toasted (see page 21)

Yield: 12 large or 24 small bars

continued →

sweet cherry crumble bars, continued

While the base is baking, prepare the topping: Pour the almonds into a small bowl. Break up the remaining 1½ cups / 300g topping dough over the almonds. Using your hands, press the almonds into the dough. Set aside.

Spread the compote over the base, leaving a ¼- to ½-inch border around the perimeter. Break the topping into uneven pieces and sprinkle it over the compote. Slide the pan into the oven and bake for 35–40 minutes, until the topping is golden in spots.

Let the bars cool completely. Use the parchment to lift them from the pan. Cut into bars (see Element 11, page 7) and serve.

The bars can be stored in an airtight container and refrigerated for up to 3 days.

maple-pecan not-pie bars

These bars are easier than a pecan pie, and they're lacking that weird sticky stuff that's found in a more traditional pecan pie. Rejoice! No weird sticky stuff. While these bars are my favorite at room temperature, I know some people who think they're better when cold from the fridge. For a true dessert, warm the bars and serve them with scoops of ice cream—the easiest "not-pie" for your next holiday dinner.

solid gold

Maple-Pecan Not-Pie Bars feature a bottom layer of dough that is baked before the filling is added. This isn't a step you should skip, because an underbaked dough base leads to a bar that's less than perfect (and a bar that can get soggy fast). With a little planning, you can prep the base of these bars ahead of time. Press the dough into the pan, then refrigerate or freeze the whole thing until you're ready to proceed with the recipe. As far as ingredients go, you could substitute honey for the maple syrup in these bars. If you make that choice, you'll have Honey-Pecan Not-Pie Bars on your hands.

Preheat the oven to 350°F. Line a 9 by 13-inch pan with parchment paper (see Element 5, page 4).

Press the dough into the prepared pan to make an even base with no cracks. Refrigerate until the dough is firm to the touch, about 15 minutes. Bake for 35–45 minutes, until the base is golden brown. The base is now ready to be topped with the filling.

Make the filling: In a medium saucepan, bring the butter, brown sugar, granulated sugar, maple syrup, heavy cream, and salt to a boil over medium heat, stirring occasionally. Add the pecans and stir. Bring back up to a boil, stir, and cook for exactly 2 minutes.

Spread the filling over the base, covering all the way to the edges of the pan and making sure the nuts and saucy stuff

4 cups / 800g Butter Dough (page 46)

Maple-Pecan Filling

½ cup / 113g unsalted butter

½ cup / 108g brown sugar

1 Tbsp / 15g granulated sugar

⅓ cup / 115g maple syrup

2 Tbsp / 30g heavy cream

½ tsp / 3g kosher salt

2½ cups / 250g pecan pieces, toasted (see page 21)

1½ tsp / 4g sea salt flakes for finishing

Yield: 12 large or 24 small bars

continued →

maple-pecan not-pie bars, continued

are evenly distributed. Slide the pan into the oven and bake for 10–12 minutes.

Let the bars cool for 5–8 minutes and then sprinkle the sea salt flakes evenly over the top. Let the bars cool in the pan for at least 1 hour, or until they reach room temperature. They'll be easier to remove from the pan and cut when they are completely cool. Using the parchment paper, transfer the slab to a cutting board. Cut into bars (see Element 11, page 7).

The bars can be stored in an airtight container at room temperature for 1 day or in the refrigerator for up to 4 days. Bring to room temperature before serving.

brown sugar-oat dough

Not only is this buttery stuff ready to become the base dough of a bevy of bars, it's also destined to top all your fruit crisps and crumbles. It's an ice cream topping, too, and is even quite nice layered into a yogurt parfait. It can become the crumb in a vanilla crumb cake and can even serve as the top crust for an apple pie. You'll want to keep your freezer stocked with this.

solid gold

A recipe using a base layer will call for about 3 cups / 585g of this dough. You can double or even triple the recipe and store the dough in resealable bags in the refrigerator for up to 1 week or in the freezer for up to 3 months. When you're ready to bake, simply pull the bag of dough from the refrigerator or freezer and remove the amount called for in the recipe you're baking, returning the bag to the refrigerator or freezer immediately.

3 cups / 360g all-purpose flour

2 cups / 200g thick rolled oats

¾ cup / 162g brown sugar

½ cup / 100g granulated sugar

1 tsp / 5g kosher salt

1 Tbsp / 18g pure vanilla extract

1½ cups / 339g unsalted butter, melted

Yield: Approximately 6 cups / 1.17kg dough

Scoop the flour, oats, both sugars, and salt into a large bowl. Stir to combine. Add the vanilla to the melted butter, then pour the melted butter over the top of the flour and oat combination. Stir until all traces of flour have disappeared and the dough is chunky and holds together when you squeeze it in your hands.

Pack into freezer bags or another airtight container, pressing it somewhat flat. Once cold, the dough will become quite stiff, and a flatter dough is easier to break apart than a large boulder.

The dough can be refrigerated for up to 4 days or frozen for up to 3 months.

Interchangeable Oats

For oat-related recipes, I always reach for rolled oats. They make the Brown Sugar–Oat Dough thick and chewy. If you have quick-cooking oats (not rolled oats) in your pantry, go ahead and use them (and add rolled oats to your shopping list for next time).

goodie snacktime bars

blueberry-coconut-orange ones

jam jambles

nutty chocolate oaties

blueberry-coconut-orange ones

Brown Sugar–Oat Dough forms the base of these bars, which are a little juicy from the blueberries and orange and a little chewy from the coconut. Destined for picnics, desk breakfasts, lunch boxes, and after-school snacks, these bars are perfect. And while they're completely enjoyable cold or at room temperature, they're even better served slightly warm with a scoop of ice cream.

solid gold

You can use blackberries here instead of blueberries. Both fresh and frozen will work, with the frozen coming in handy if you're baking these in winter. Even when it's not winter, I like to bake with frozen fruit. It's easy, cuts down on prep time, and the quality of the fruit is generally reliable.

Make the topping: Combine the berries, coconut, sugar, and orange zest and juice in a medium saucepan. Bring to a simmer over medium heat. Allow the berries to cook for 12 minutes, or until they're a bit broken down and very juicy. Remove the pan from the heat. The berries are ready to use immediately or can be refrigerated, airtight, for up to 5 days.

Preheat the oven to 350°F. Line a 9 by 13-inch pan with parchment paper (see Element 5, page 4).

Press about 4 cups / 780g of the dough into the prepared pan. The dough should be pressed nice and tight with no cracks. Bake for about 30 minutes, until the edges of the dough are golden.

Using a large slotted spoon, scoop the berries onto the top of the base, leaving most of their juice behind. Crumble the remaining 2 cups / 390g dough over the blueberries, leaving blue peeking through. Slide the pan back into the oven and bake for about 30 minutes, until the topping is pale golden brown and looks dry.

Let the bars cool to room temperature. Use the parchment to lift the bars from the pan. Cut into bars (see Element 11, page 7). The bars will keep for up to 2 days, well wrapped, at room temperature. They can also be wrapped and frozen for up to 1 month. Unwrap and bring to room temperature before serving.

Blueberry-Coconut-Orange Topping

4 cups / 460g frozen or fresh blueberries

¾ cup / 65g sweetened, shredded coconut

½ cup / 100g granulated sugar

Grated zest and juice of 1 orange

1 recipe Brown Sugar–Oat Dough (page 74)

Yield: 12 large or 24 small bars

goodie snacktime bars

Once upon a time I was very serious about making snacks for my kid. I'd whip up snacky foods for fun, sending him off to school with a jackpot of all-handmade delights: Heart-shaped cheese crackers, fortune cookies filled with custom fortunes, peanut-butter-and-jelly sushi rolls, and fruit leather made with berries from our yard. While I've lost my knack for intensive snack prep, these bars have somehow managed to stay on my baking list. They're easy to bake, and when cut and wrapped individually they're the ideal treat to grab on the way to school or work. (Pictured on page 76)

solid gold

Goodie Snacktime Bars are endlessly customizable. I like to make them with white chocolate, cherries, and toffee, for certain. That said, if you love butterscotch chips and coconut, by all means use those (see the variation that follows). If you'd rather go with peanut butter chips and raisins with a sprinkle of cinnamon, be my guest. Make these bars your own.

Preheat the oven to 350°F. Line a 9 by 13-inch pan with parchment paper (see Element 5, page 4).

Place the dough in a mixing bowl. Add the white chocolate chips and cherries. Mix with your hands until the chocolate and cherries are evenly distributed.

Press the dough into the prepared pan, fitting it snugly into the corners and forming an even base with no cracks. Sprinkle the toffee bits all over the top of the dough.

Bake for 40–45 minutes, until the edges are golden and slightly firmer than the center.

Allow the bars to cool completely, then use the parchment paper to lift them out of the pan. Cut into bars (see Element 11, page 7).

The bars can be stored in an airtight container at room temperature for 1 day or in the refrigerator for up to 5 days. Bring to room temperature before serving.

4 cups / 780g Brown Sugar–Oat Dough (page 74)

1 cup / 170g white chocolate chips

1 cup / 150g dried cherries

½ cup / 100g toffee bits (plain toffee, sometimes called Bits o' Brickle, not chocolate coated; see facing page)

Yield: 12 large or 24 small bars

Baking Gold Reinventions

Peanut Butter, Raisin, Cinnamon Goodie Snacktime Bars

Use 1 cup / 170g peanut butter chips, 1 cup / 150g raisins, and 2 tsp / 4g ground cinnamon in place of the white chocolate and cherries called for in the recipe. Mix the dough and press it into the pan as directed, omitting the toffee bits sprinkled on top. Bake as directed.

Butterscotch, Cashew, Coconut Goodie Snacktime Bars

Use 1 cup / 170g butterscotch chips, 1 cup / 113g chopped cashews, and 1 cup / 85g sweetened, shredded coconut in place of the white chocolate and cherries called for in the recipe. Mix the dough and press it into the pan as directed, omitting the toffee bits sprinkled on top. Bake as directed.

Chocolate, Peanut, Sea Salt Goodie Snacktime Bars

Use 1 cup / 170g chocolate chips, 1 cup / 140g peanuts, and 2 tsp / 6g sea salt in place of the white chocolate and cherries called for in the recipe. Mix the dough and press it into the pan as directed, omitting the toffee bits sprinkled on top. Bake as directed.

Toffee Bits, Explained

Take note! All toffee bits are not the same. The toffee bits called for in *Baking Gold* recipes are the type that are not coated in chocolate. The package may say "English Toffee Bits o' Brickle," and that's exactly what you're looking for. Always use toffee bits that are nothing more than toffee.

nutty chocolate oaties

These bars are chocolatey, crunchy, crispy, buttery, and coconutty. They're great with milk, practically scream for ice cream, and would even be a great match for slightly sweetened whipped cream. If you're looking for an ice cream sundae that's crazy good, try chopping these bars, layering them into a parfait glass with vanilla ice cream, and topping the whole delight with a spoonful or two of warm Cocoa Fudge Sauce (page 103). (Pictured on page 76.)

solid gold

There's a welcome layer of chocolate in these bars that makes its way there using a little trick I love. The chocolate is sprinkled on the partially baked base, then the pan goes into the oven for a very few minutes. The pan emerges, the chocolate is melty and spreadable, and you skip the stovetop or microwave melting of chocolate, which means time saved and fewer dishes!

Preheat the oven to 350°F. Line a 9 by 13-inch pan with parchment paper (see Element 5, page 4).

Press the dough into the prepared pan, fitting it snugly into the corners and forming an even base with no cracks. Bake for 17–20 minutes, until the edges are golden.

Remove the pan from the oven and immediately sprinkle the chocolate over the baked base. Return the pan to the oven for 3 minutes to melt the chocolate. Remove the pan from the oven and spread the chocolate evenly over the base. Set the pan aside and give the chocolate 10–15 minutes to cool and set.

Place the brown sugar and salt in a bowl and stir until the salt is no longer visible. Add the sweetened condensed milk, egg yolks, and vanilla and stir again. Next, add the coconut, oats, and pecans and stir to combine (the mixture will be very thick, like a cookie dough). Once everything comes together in what looks like an evenly mixed dough, you're ready to get it in the pan. Use your hands to distribute the topping evenly over the melted chocolate.

½ recipe Brown Sugar–Oat Dough (page 74)

8 oz / 227g chocolate (see Element 7, page 5, for tips on using the chocolate you have), chopped

1½ cups / 325g brown sugar

2 tsp / 10g kosher salt

½ cup / 110g sweetened condensed milk

2 large egg yolks, beaten

1 Tbsp / 18g pure vanilla extract

1½ cups / 130g sweetened, shredded coconut, toasted (see page 22)

⅓ cup / 33g rolled oats

1¾ cups / 175g pecan pieces, toasted

Yield: 12 large or 24 small bars

Bake the bars for 25–28 minutes, until set yet still soft. The bars will have taken on a golden hue. They are always better a little underbaked rather than a little overbaked.

Let the bars cool in the pan to room temperature. Use the parchment paper to lift the bars out of the pan and transfer them to a cutting board. Cut into bars (see Element 11, page 7). Store the bars at room temperature, well wrapped, for up to 4 days.

apple-citrus crisp

Brown Sugar–Oat Dough was born to be baked atop a bed of apples. Here the apples combine with a bit of lemon zest to create an apple crisp you're going to come back to time and again because it tastes exactly the way you want apple crisp to taste (and it's extremely easy). You can use any apples you like to eat—tart or sweet or a mix. And it's always a bright idea to have vanilla ice cream in the freezer when you make this. And if you've got thick yogurt in the refrigerator? I suggest breakfast.

solid gold

Let's talk apple sizes. I call for medium apples in this recipe. A medium apple is approximately 2¾ inches in diameter. Can you use larger apples? Certainly! This crisp is forgiving, and it won't matter if you use a few too many apple slices (or a few too few, for that matter).

Preheat the oven to 350°F. Butter the sides and bottom of a 9 by 13-inch pan.

Place the apple slices in a bowl. Add the sugars, cinnamon, and lemon zest and juice and toss to coat the slices. Pour the apples into the prepared pan.

Crumble the dough over the top of the apples. Bake for about 1 hour, until the topping is golden brown and the apples are bubbling thickly.

Serve warm, spooned into bowls. The crisp can be covered and refrigerated for up to 5 days.

Baking Gold Reinventions

Apple-Vanilla Crisp

Omit the lemon zest and juice. Add 1 Tbsp / 18g pure vanilla extract, plus the scraped-out seeds of a vanilla bean to the apple slices. Toss to distribute the vanilla seeds. Bake as directed.

12 medium apples, peeled, cored, and sliced

½ cup / 108g brown sugar

½ cup / 100g granulated sugar

2 tsp / 4g ground cinnamon

Grated zest and juice of 1 lemon

1 recipe Brown Sugar–Oat Dough (page 74)

Yield: 9 by 13-inch crisp

continued →

apple-citrus crisp, continued

Spiced Apple Crisp

Substitute the granulated sugar and cinnamon called for in the recipe with ½ cup / 100g Bubble Bun Dust (page 29). Eliminate the lemon zest and juice. Bake as directed.

Apple-Cherry Crisp with Almonds

Add 1 cup / 150g dried cherries when tossing the apple slices with the sugars and cinnamon. Eliminate the lemon zest and juice. After crumbling the dough over the apples, sprinkle ½ cup / 60g slivered almonds over top. Bake as directed.

Peach-Blackberry Crisp

Replace the apples with approximately 8 cups / 1.2kg peaches or nectarines (frozen or fresh, sliced) plus approximately 2 cups / 300g blackberries (frozen or fresh). Omit the lemon zest and juice. If using frozen fruit, no need to thaw. Bake as directed.

apricot-walnut caramel tarts with honey cream

These tiny tarts are a true sensation—full of amazing flavor and terrific textures. The crunch of the tart dough, the chew of the apricots, the smoothness of the caramel—it's almost too much. Make these for a party or as the big finish to a special dinner. Or, be like me, and make them because you can.

solid gold

For this tart, don't use the dried apricots you found in your pantry that may or may not be from your last road trip two summers ago. Same for the nuts—if you can't remember when you bought the walnuts, I'd advise you to not use them. There really aren't that many ingredients in this tart, so you want the ones you use to be worth eating.

Make the caramel: Prepare a double boiler or set a heatproof bowl over (but not touching) a pan of simmering water. Pour the sweetened condensed milk into the top of the double boiler. Turn the stove to high and bring the water in the double boiler to a full boil. Lower the heat to medium-high and add the apricots and walnuts, stirring to distribute. Cover the top of the double boiler and allow the sweetened condensed milk to cook until caramelized, stirring every 30 minutes or so, for about 90 minutes total. Check the water level when you stir and add more as needed. The milk will thicken and become darker in color—a sort of golden caramel shade. Once it has caramelized, turn off the heat and leave the double boiler on the stove for 10 minutes. The caramel is now ready to use.

Preheat the oven to 350°F.

Press 2 Tbsp / 20g dough into the bottom of 16 wells of the muffin pans, pressing firmly and evenly.

continued →

Apricot-Walnut Caramel

1 (14 oz / 396g) can sweetened condensed milk

½ cup / 90g dried apricots, chopped

½ cup / 50g walnuts, chopped

About 2 cups / 320g Brown Sugar–Oat Dough (page 74)

Sea salt flakes for sprinkling

Honey Cream

½ cup / 120g heavy cream

2 tsp / 14g honey

Yield: 16 tiny tarts

apricot-walnut caramel tarts
with honey cream, continued

Bake for 15–20 minutes, until the dough is golden at the edges. Let the bases cool completely, then carefully remove them from the muffin pans.

Top each of the tart bases with a spoonful of the caramel. Sprinkle with sea salt.

Make the honey cream: In a large bowl, combine the cream and honey. Using a whisk or a hand mixer, whip until soft peaks form. Top the tarts with a spoonful of the whipped cream. Serve immediately.

The tarts can be made ahead up to the point you sprinkle them with salt. Store in an airtight container for up to 3 days. Top with the whipped cream right before you're ready to serve.

2 Batters

Cake! For too long I thought I hated cake. Then I opened a bakery and was surprised to discover that the majority of cake I had been eating was the wrong cake. Enter sour cream cake batter, which makes the right cake—cake that I love.

Give me that Peanut Butter–Fudge Polka Dot Cake from page 103 any day of the week and I will eat the entire thing by myself in no time flat. Probably not the greatest thing to admit, I know. Still, if I can't be honest with you about my cake-eating ability, who else is there?

Vanilla–Sour Cream Batter changed me from someone who only ever wanted chocolate cake to someone who actually enjoys vanilla cake. I love the Cinnamon Crumble Cake (page 126) because the recipe is so unexpected. How does Brown Sugar–Oat Dough combined with cake batter become a first-rate coffee cake–type delight? A baking mystery I've happily solved.

What makes these batters pure Baking Gold? Ultra-easy cake baking! My friends get worked up about cake. They tell me that cake-making is stressful, it makes them nervous, and the cakes never turn out. I'm here to eliminate those feelings. With Baking Gold, cakes are nearly carefree. You can deck out these cakes with the simplest of decorations—nothing fussy required. I love to eliminate cake-making worries and help people create incredible cakes. And I love to keep it simple by baking all of my cakes in a 9 by 13-inch pan.

chocolate-sour cream batter

Chocolate cake is my favorite cake, and this chocolate batter makes the cake I love more than all other chocolate cakes. It works with everything from a simple chocolate glaze to a thick layer of peanut butter buttercream. It also works with any sort of cream cheese buttercream and (big secret) it's a total treat to eat it frozen (yes, even plain!).

solid gold

One look at this recipe and you see it's not a typical batter. In a move that's a bit dated (my grandma made cakes using batters like these), the typical fat-as-butter is replaced with fat-as-oil. And then there's boiling liquid! Why? Because the oil allows you to skip time-consuming steps like creaming butter and sugar. And the boiling (not merely hot) coffee makes it possible to add all the ingredients at once—the heat of the boiling coffee softens and melts the other ingredients into a batter. The basic steps of this recipe are easy enough that I dare say *everyone* is capable of baking it.

Preheat the oven to 350°F. Line a 9 by 13-inch pan with parchment paper (see Element 5, page 4).

Combine the sugar, flour, cocoa powder, baking soda, baking powder, and salt in a large bowl. Use a sturdy spoon to stir them all together.

In a medium bowl, combine the eggs and sour cream with a fork, mixing until smooth. Add the oil and vanilla and use the fork to mix until they're incorporated. The mixture will be smooth and creamy.

Add the wet ingredients to the dry ingredients and stir to combine. The batter will turn very thick.

Add the coffee in thirds, stirring after each addition. Once all the coffee has been added, continue stirring until the batter is smooth and has thinned slightly with no traces of unmixed ingredients remaining.

2 cups / 400g granulated sugar

2 cups / 240g all-purpose flour

1 cup / 100g cocoa powder

2 tsp / 12g baking soda

2 tsp / 8g baking powder

1 tsp / 5g kosher salt

2 large eggs

1 cup / 227g sour cream

½ cup / 105g canola oil

2 tsp / 12g pure vanilla extract

1 cup / 230g boiling coffee in a glass measuring cup

Yield: 9 by 13-inch cake

Pour the batter into the prepared pan and bake for 35–40 minutes, until the cake is springy to the touch and a toothpick inserted into the middle comes out clean (or barely smudged with chocolate). Let the cake cool completely before assembling and decorating.

Top That Cake

It's very difficult for me to tell you how much buttercream you need to top a cake. Why? Because I lack buttercream control. I'll pile it on thick with zero worries. That said, in my professional opinion, all of the buttercream recipes in *Baking Gold* yield the perfect amount for a cake baked in a 9 by 13-inch pan. If you prefer less, by all means, use less.

Baking Time

 9-inch cake rounds: Bake 30–35 minutes at 350°F

 9 by 13-inch cake: Bake 40 minutes at 350°F

 Standard cupcakes: Bake 15–18 minutes at 350°F

everyday chocolate cake

Is every day a cake day? It's possible with this cake! Cake for no reason at all quickly turns a regular weeknight into an impromptu party for everyone around the table. And that's what I like about a cake like this—no special occasion necessary, easy enough to whip up after work, and a total surprise for those least expecting it.

solid gold

If you're short on time to make cake, you still have time to make this one. Here's how: First, you can bake the cake a day ahead. Mix the batter, bake, and leave the cake to cool in the pan. Once it's completely cool, wrap it airtight and store it at room temperature. The following day, simply top the cake with buttercream and sprinkles. You'll never be able to tell that the cake itself is a day old.

Preheat the oven to 350°F. Line a 9 by 13-inch pan with parchment paper (see Element 5, page 4).

Pour the batter into the prepared pan and bake for 35–40 minutes, until the cake is springy to the touch and a toothpick inserted into the middle comes out clean (or barely smudged with chocolate). Let the cake cool completely.

Make the buttercream: Put the cream cheese in the bowl of a stand mixer fitted with the paddle attachment. Mix on medium speed for 30 seconds to 1 minute, until the cream cheese is smooth. Add the butter and mix on medium again, until the butter and cream cheese come together and look creamy. Check for lumps of either butter or cream cheese and mix until you no longer see them. It's easiest to rid the buttercream of lumps now rather than at the end of mixing. Scrape the bottom and sides of the bowl.

Add the vanilla and mix for about 10 seconds, until you no longer see traces of it.

● 1 recipe Chocolate–Sour Cream Batter (page 96)

Cream Cheese Buttercream

16 oz / 454g cream cheese, at room temperature

1½ cups / 339g unsalted butter, at room temperature

2 tsp / 12g pure vanilla extract

5 cups / 565g powdered sugar, sifted

1 Tbsp / 14g sour cream

Sprinkles of choice

Yield: 9 by 13-inch cake

continued →

Add the powdered sugar in thirds, mixing on low and waiting until each addition is fully mixed in and scraping the sides of the bowl between each addition. Once all the powdered sugar has been added, scrape the sides and bottom of the bowl to incorporate any unmixed ingredients.

Add the sour cream and mix for a few seconds.

The buttercream is ready to use right away, or it can be covered tightly and refrigerated for 3–4 days. If you've refrigerated it, let it come to room temperature, give it a stir, and it will be ready to use.

Cover the top of the cake in Cream Cheese Buttercream. I like to use the full recipe for a perfectly thick layer. You may choose to use less—this is your everyday cake. And don't forget the sprinkles! Decorate the top with custom sprinkles (see page 200), rainbow jimmies, or tiny nonpareils.

Covered, the cake can be kept on your countertop at cool room temperature for 1 day. It will keep for up to 5 days if well wrapped and refrigerated, although it's most enjoyable to eat at room temperature.

the perfect temp

The temperature of the butter and cream cheese really matters, when making Cream Cheese Buttercream. Ideally, their temperatures should match—one should not be firmer than the other. Press a finger into the butter and then press a finger into the cream cheese—using the same pressure, the butter and cream cheese should feel the same when pressed. If one is colder than the other, they won't blend as well and you'll end up with lumpy buttercream. And no one wants lumpy buttercream.

peanut butter-fudge polka dot cake

This is my cake. It's the cake I want to bake, it's the cake I want to eat, it's the cake I bake for birthdays, anniversaries, and tiny celebrations that call for cake. It's easy, the components can all be made ahead (which means you can pull this off with minimal work on cake day!), and it's very good. How good is this cake? My friends tell me they have dreams about it, that's how good it is.

solid gold

The superstar components of this cake are Chocolate–Sour Cream batter, Peanut Butter Buttercream, and Cocoa Fudge Sauce. Separately, they shine. Together? They make a cake that is out of this world. You start with the cake. Then the buttercream goes on the cake. Then the fudge sauce goes on top of the buttercream. Note: You want to make sure the fudge sauce doesn't melt the buttercream. The key to this is to have the buttercream cold (hence the 20-minute rest in the fridge). The sauce is pourable and barely warm to the touch. If you've made the sauce in advance, a double boiler makes warming it easy. The sauce is ready to use when it's still kind of thick yet pourable.

Preheat the oven to 350°F. Line a 9 by 13-inch pan with parchment paper (see Element 5, page 4).

Pour the batter into the prepared pan and bake for 35–40 minutes, until the cake is springy to the touch and a toothpick inserted into the middle comes out clean (or barely smudged with chocolate). Let the cake cool completely.

Make the buttercream: In a stand mixer fitted with the paddle attachment, beat together the peanut butter, butter, and cream cheese until smooth, creamy, and evenly mixed. With the mixer on low, add the powdered sugar, a bit at a time, and mix until you no longer see traces of it. Stop the mixer and scrape the bottom and sides of the bowl. Add the vanilla and salt and mix on medium until the buttercream is light and fluffy, about

continued →

1 recipe Chocolate–Sour Cream Batter (page 96)

Peanut Butter Buttercream

1½ cups / 405g peanut butter, at room temperature

1½ cups / 339g unsalted butter, at room temperature

¼ cup / 57g cream cheese, at room temperature

1⅓ cups / 156g powdered sugar, sifted

1 tsp / 6g pure vanilla extract

1 tsp / 5g kosher salt

Cocoa Fudge Sauce

1 cup / 240g heavy cream

½ cup / 113g unsalted butter

1 cup / 215g brown sugar

½ cup / 100g granulated sugar

½ tsp / 3g kosher salt

1⅓ cups / 130g cocoa powder

2 tsp / 12g pure vanilla extract

Yield: 9 by 13-inch cake

peanut butter–fudge polka dot cake, continued

2 minutes. Transfer the buttercream to a clean bowl, cover, and refrigerate until it's firm enough to scoop, 20–30 minutes. The buttercream can also be stored in an airtight container at cool room temperature for up to 1 day or in the refrigerator for up to 1 week. If you've refrigerated it, let it come to a scoopable consistency and proceed with the directions for scooping the buttercream onto the cake.

Make the fudge sauce: In a medium saucepan, combine the cream, butter, brown sugar, granulated sugar, and salt. Bring to a simmer over medium heat and stir as the butter melts. Once the contents of the pan are simmering, continue to simmer for 2 minutes. Remove the pan from the heat and add the cocoa powder, whisking until smooth. Whisk in the vanilla. Transfer the sauce to a clean bowl and let cool until it's thick yet pourable and barely warm to the touch. The sauce can also be covered and refrigerated for up to 1 week, then rewarmed slightly in a double boiler (until thick yet pourable).

Using a 2 Tbsp / 30ml scoop, scoop the buttercream onto the cake, flat-side down. Continue scooping, in a pattern or randomly, until you've scooped all the buttercream onto the cake. When you're finished, the cake will look like it has polka dots of peanut butter buttercream all over the top. Refrigerate the cake until the buttercream mounds are firm to the touch, approximately 20 minutes. Once the buttercream is firm, you're ready to pour on the fudge sauce. Starting at one end of the cake, slowly pour the Chocolate Fudge Sauce over the top, coating all the little hills of buttercream as evenly as you can. Let the cake rest until the glaze has cooled.

Covered, the cake can be kept on your countertop at cool room temperature for 1 day. It will keep for up to 5 days if well wrapped and refrigerated, although it's most enjoyable to eat at room temperature.

Baking Gold Reinvention

Cocoa Fudge–Glazed Peanut Butter Cake

Flip things around and start with the sauce first: After the cake has cooled, pour the Cocoa Fudge Sauce over the top. Allow it to cool and set. Spread a thick layer of Peanut Butter Buttercream over the top of the fudge. Leave plain or top with sprinkles, crumbled cookies, or mini marshmallows.

chocolate-peppermint cake

This cake forces me to ask a question: Would Santa like cake rather than (yet another) plate of cookies? If your answer is yes, then this is the cake he deserves to have waiting for him after his big squeeze down the chimney. I love to top this cake with bits and pieces of peppermint ribbon candy. You can do the same, or you can opt for crushed candy canes or another minty hard candy of your choice.

solid gold

Infusing milk or cream with tea for flavoring buttercreams, whipped creams, ice cream, milk, and more is one of my favorite tricks. It's a simple matter of steeping tea bags in steamy milk, cooling the milk, then using it in place of regular milk in recipes. In addition to mint tea, I love using Earl Grey, chai, and even English Breakfast or chamomile.

Preheat the oven to 350°F. Line a 9 by 13-inch pan with parchment paper (see Element 5, page 4).

Pour the batter into the prepared pan and bake for 35–40 minutes, until the cake is springy to the touch and a toothpick inserted into the middle comes out clean (or barely smudged with chocolate). Let the cake cool completely.

Make the buttercream: Pour the milk into a small saucepan. Add the tea bags. Bring the milk to a simmer over low heat, until it is steamy and you see tiny bubbles on the surface of the milk.

Transfer the hot milk and tea bags to a clean bowl and refrigerate until completely cold. Remove the tea bags from the milk and it's ready to use.

Place the butter in the bowl of a stand mixer fitted with the paddle attachment. Beat the butter on medium speed until smooth, 3–5 minutes. Scrape the bowl, then add the powdered sugar and vanilla. Mix on low. With the mixer running, add the

1 recipe Chocolate–Sour Cream Batter (page 96)

Peppermint Buttercream

½ cup plus 2 tablespoons / 142g whole milk

3 bags peppermint tea

1 cup / 226g unsalted butter, at room temperature

11 cups / 1.25kg powdered sugar, sifted

1 Tbsp / 18g pure vanilla extract

Up to 1½ cups / 280g whole, broken, or crushed peppermint ribbon candy or candy canes

Yield: 9 by 13-inch cake or 12 (2¾-inch) round pieces

continued →

minty milk, a little at a time. The sugar will reduce in volume and the contents of the mixer will start to look like buttercream. Keep mixing until the buttercream is smooth and spreadable and not at all runny.

The buttercream is ready to use. You can keep the buttercream in an airtight container at room temperature for up to 2 days or in the refrigerator for up to 1 week. To use buttercream that has been refrigerated, let it come to room temperature. Give the buttercream a good stir with a sturdy spoon before using.

Once the cake has cooled, cover it in a wonderfully thick layer of Peppermint Buttercream. Sprinkle the bits and pieces of peppermint ribbon candy over the top. When I'm feeling a little fancy, I like to cut this cake into round pieces before covering it with the buttercream and bits of candy. To make it easy, I lift the whole cake out of the pan and place it on a cutting board. Then I use a 2¾-inch round cutter to punch out 12 round pieces. Once cut, I pipe or spread on buttercream and top with candy. For more easy "fancy" cake ideas, see page 120.

Covered, the cake can be kept on your countertop at cool room temperature for 1 day. It will keep for up to 5 days if well wrapped and refrigerated, although it's most enjoyable to eat at room temperature.

chocolate-cherry cake

This cake is a great example of Baking Gold. It seems complicated (your friends and family will assume you took the day off to bake it), however it's not at all if you have the main components of the cake—chocolate cake, cherry buttercream, and cherry compote—ready to go.

solid gold

Another trick I highly recommend is mixing fruit into Cream Cheese Buttercream to make fruity buttercream. Chocolate-Cherry Cake wouldn't be the same without the Sweet Cherry Compote (page 68) stirred into Cream Cheese Buttercream that you've already made. The cherries make the buttercream a very pretty pink color, and you can pluck a few extra cherries from the compote to bedazzle the top of the cake with once it's covered in the buttercream.

Preheat the oven to 350°F. Line a 9 by 13-inch pan with parchment paper (see Element 5, page 4).

Pour the batter into the prepared pan and bake for 35–40 minutes, until the cake is springy to the touch and a toothpick inserted into the middle comes out clean (or barely smudged with chocolate). Let the cake cool completely.

Make the buttercream: The softness of the butter and cream cheese really matter here. Ideally, they should match in softness. If they aren't equally soft, it will be difficult to cream them together without them being lumpy.

Put the cream cheese in the bowl of a stand mixer fitted with the paddle attachment. Mix on medium speed for 30 seconds to 1 minute, until the cream cheese is smooth. Add the butter and mix on medium again, until the butter and cream cheese come together and look creamy. Check for lumps of either butter or cream cheese and mix until you no longer see them. It's easiest to rid the buttercream of lumps now rather than at the end of mixing. Scrape the bottom and sides of the bowl.

1 recipe Chocolate–Sour Cream Batter (page 96)

Cherry-Cream Cheese Buttercream

16 oz / 454g cream cheese, at soft room temperature

1½ cups / 339g unsalted butter, at soft room temperature

2 tsp / 12g pure vanilla extract

5 cups / 567g powdered sugar, sifted

1 Tbsp / 14g sour cream

About ¼ cup / 85g Sweet Cherry Compote (page 68)

12 whole cherries or large cherry pieces from the compote, patted dry

Yield: 9 by 13-inch cake

continued →

chocolate-cherry cake, continued

Add the vanilla and mix for about 10 seconds, until you no longer see traces of it.

Add the powdered sugar in thirds, mixing on low and waiting until each addition is fully mixed in and scraping the sides of the bowl between each addition.

Once all the powdered sugar is added, scrape the bowl again with no traces of unmixed ingredients remaining. If you find any, mix to incorporate.

Add the sour cream and mix for a few seconds. Remove the bowl from the mixer and add the cherry compote. Stir the compote into the buttercream—it will turn pale pink and you'll see the cherries evenly distributed.

The buttercream can be used immediately or covered tightly and refrigerated for 3–4 days. To use buttercream that has been refrigerated, let it come to room temperature. Give the buttercream a good stir with a sturdy spoon before using.

Smooth the buttercream over the cake, swirling it around as much as you'd like. Finish with the reserved cherries, dotting the top of the cake with them.

Covered, the cake can be kept on your countertop at cool room temperature for 1 day. It will keep for up to 5 days if well wrapped and refrigerated, although it's most enjoyable to eat at room temperature.

marshmallow-cocoa cake

Deep dark chocolate cake. A layer of fudge. A layer of marshmallow. More marshmallows. This cake! It's the kind of thing you eat and then wonder how and when you can get more. Downright decadent, this is a special cake for special occasions (even if your special occasion is a regular Saturday afternoon).

solid gold

If you're like me and you love making marshmallows, by all means use the homemade version here. Otherwise, next time you're at the market, snag a bag of the puffy stuff from the baking aisle for this recipe. The marshmallow glaze is born for cake, and it also makes what could be your favorite ice cream topping. Unmelted mini marshmallows in the glaze give the top of the cake a bumpy look that I love.

Preheat the oven to 350°F. Line a 9 by 13-inch pan with parchment paper (see Element 5, page 4).

Pour the batter into the prepared pan and bake for 35–40 minutes, until the cake is springy to the touch and a toothpick inserted into the middle comes out clean (or barely smudged with chocolate). Let the cake cool completely.

Pour the fudge sauce evenly over the top of the cake and set aside for 10–20 minutes to set.

When the fudge sauce has set for 10 minutes, make the glaze: In a double boiler or a bowl set over (but not touching) a pan of simmering water, heat 4 cups / 220g of the mini marshmallows, the half-and-half, butter, and vanilla, stirring until smooth. Let cool for approximately 10 minutes. Stir in the remaining 1 cup / 55g mini marshmallows. They should stud the glaze, not melt into it. The glaze is ready to use immediately.

Pour the marshmallow glaze over the fudge sauce–covered cake. Go slowly, pouring as evenly as possible, being mindful of the unmelted marshmallows throughout. The sauce will have a

continued →

1 recipe Chocolate–Sour Cream Cake (page 96)

1 recipe Cocoa Fudge Sauce (page 103), warmed until pourable

Marshmallow Glaze

About 5 cups / 275g mini marshmallows

3 Tbsp / 45g half-and-half or whole milk

2 Tbsp / 28g unsalted butter

1 tsp / 6g pure vanilla extract

Powdered sugar for dusting (optional)

Yield: 9 by 13-inch cake

marshmallow-cocoa cake, continued

beautiful shiny look. You can always sift a flurry of powdered sugar on top if you prefer that sort of marshmallowy matte-finish look. The cake is ready to serve and is easiest cut with a hot, dry knife.

Covered, the cake can be kept on your countertop at cool room temperature for 1 day. It will keep for up to 5 days if well wrapped and refrigerated, although it's most enjoyable to eat at room temperature.

vanilla-sour cream batter

This batter makes the vanilla cake that changed me from an all-chocolate-cake-all-the-time kind of cake person to someone who genuinely enjoys vanilla cake. Vanilla-Sour Cream Batter can be dressed up with buttercream and sprinkles for birthdays or covered in crunchy streusel as a coffee cake.

solid gold

Every baker needs a cake like this on their side. It's easy to make, limitless in variation, and the flavor is perfectly vanilla. It's not overwhelming or wacky and it works well for any cake you're trying to bake. You can experiment by stirring swirls of spices, chocolate chips, fruit, jam and more right into the batter. You can make almost any flavor of cake you'd like!

Preheat the oven to 350°F. Line a 9 by 13-inch pan with parchment paper (see Element 5, page 4).

Combine the flour, sugar, baking powder, and salt in a large bowl. Use a sturdy spoon to stir them all together.

In a medium bowl, combine the eggs and sour cream with a fork, mixing until smooth. Add the oil and vanilla and use the fork to mix until they're incorporated. The mixture will be smooth and creamy.

Add the wet ingredients to the dry ingredients and continue to stir until the dry ingredients are mostly incorporated. The batter will turn very thick.

Add the boiling water and stir until the batter is smooth and uniform with no traces of unmixed ingredients remaining.

Pour the batter into the prepared pan and bake for 35–40 minutes, until the cake is springy to the touch and a toothpick inserted into

continued →

3⅓ cups / 400g all-purpose flour

2 cups / 400g granulated sugar

1 Tbsp plus 2 tsp / 20g baking powder

1 tsp / 5g kosher salt

2 large eggs

1 cup / 227g sour cream

½ cup / 105g canola oil

1 Tbsp / 18g pure vanilla extract

⅓ cup / 75g boiling water

Yield: 9 by 13-inch cake

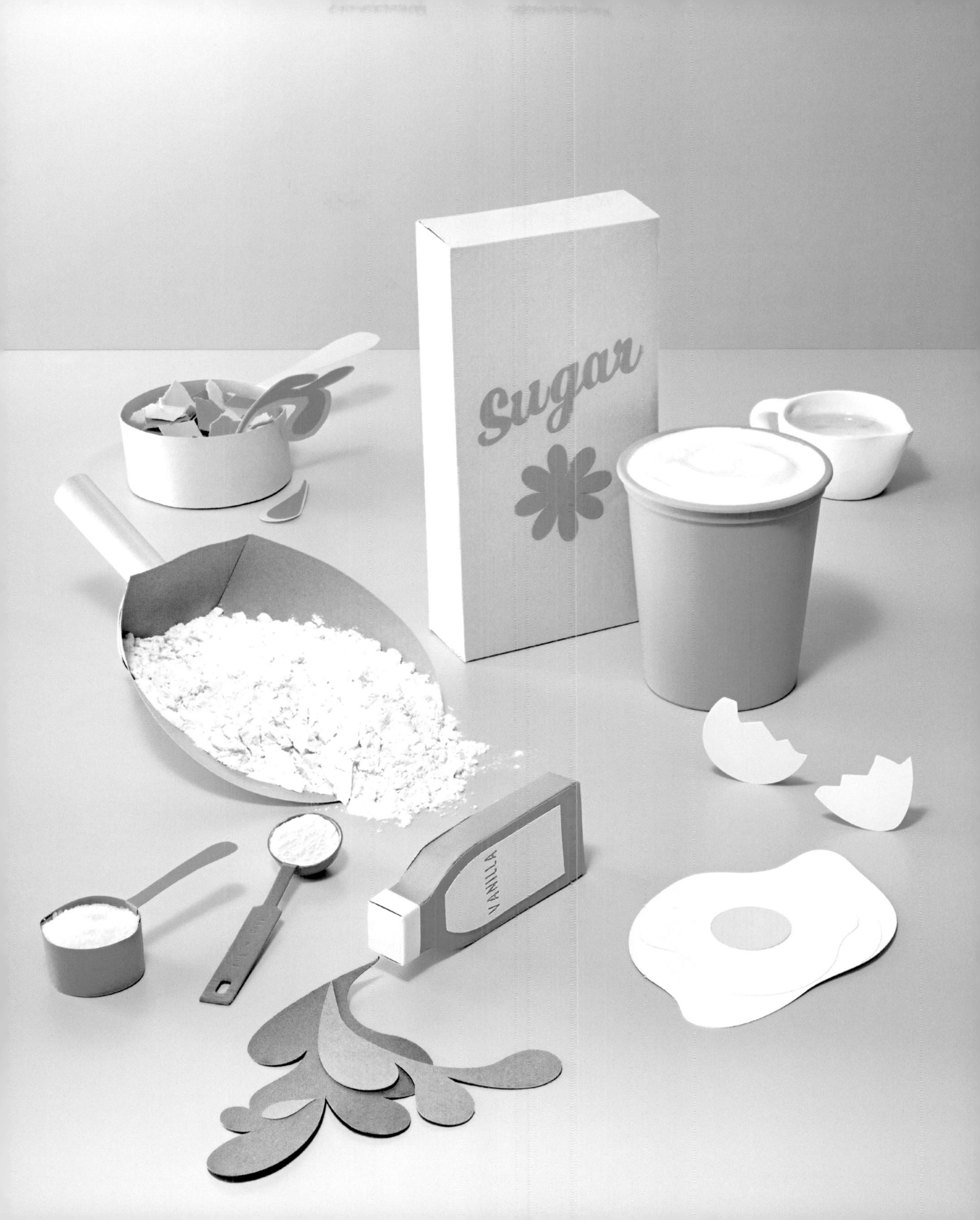
Sugar
VANILLA

vanilla-sour cream batter, continued

the middle comes out clean. Let the cake cool completely before assembling and decorating.

Covered, the cake can be stored at room temperature for up to 2 days. Wrapped and refrigerated, the cake will keep for up to 1 week.

easiest "fancy" cakes

For casual cake occasions, like when I'm serving Everyday Chocolate Cake on a random Wednesday, I like to cover the cake with buttercream (and sprinkles) when it's in the pan. It makes everything easy—especially when wrapping it to enjoy next-day leftovers. That said, there are some cake occasions that call for something fancier. And on those days, thanks to the parchment paper–lined pan, I lift the cake out, set it on a platter or cutting board, and fancy it up. For Chocolate-Cherry Cake (page 111) I like to remove the cake from the pan and cut it into squares. I pipe the buttercream onto the individual squares and top each with a cherry from the compote. For Chocolate-Peppermint Cake (page 107) and Fun Time Surprise Cake (page 132), I get even fancier and use a round cutter to cut the cake into round pieces, then I pipe or spread on buttercream and decorate. Another idea that really gets a crowd going is to serve the cake completely unadorned with buttercream and sprinkles on the side. People love to bedazzle their own cake.

vanilla celebration cake

If you've got a birthday coming up and you're in the mood for a quintessential birthday cake, do yourself a favor and make this. With its special chocolate buttercream and sprinkles, this cake is a true celebration.

solid gold

The chocolate buttercream featured in this recipe would be a winner on a chocolate cake or banana bread. It'd make a knockout sandwich cookie filling. I add sour cream to the buttercream because of its ability to take the edge off of the sweetness while adding a creamy tang. This buttercream wouldn't be the same without the sour cream—don't skip it.

Preheat the oven to 350°F. Line a 9 by 13-inch pan with parchment paper (see Element 5, page 4).

Pour the batter into the prepared pan and use a spatula to smooth it evenly into the corners.

Bake for 35–40 minutes, until the cake is springy to the touch and a toothpick inserted into the center comes out clean. Let the cake cool completely.

Make the buttercream: In the bowl of a stand mixer fitted with the paddle attachment, cream together the butter and brown sugar until they're light and fluffy. Add the powdered sugar and mix on low until gravelly. Turn the mixer off and scrape the bottom and sides of the bowl.

In a small bowl, combine the cocoa powder, salt, cinnamon, and sour cream. The sour cream will turn into little blobs in the cocoa powder, and that's okay. Add this to the mixer bowl and mix to combine. Scrape the bottom and sides of the bowl.

Add the vanilla and mix until the contents look wet and dark.

With the mixer on low, add the milk a splash at a time. After all of the milk has been added, stop the mixer and scrape the bowl again. Turn the mixer to medium and whip the buttercream for about 1 minute.

1 recipe Vanilla–Sour Cream Batter (page 118)

Special Chocolate Buttercream

1 cup / 226g unsalted butter, at room temperature

¼ cup / 54g brown sugar

3 cups / 340g powdered sugar, sifted

1 cup / 100g cocoa powder

½ tsp / 3g kosher salt

½ tsp / 1g ground cinnamon

¼ cup / 57g sour cream

1 Tbsp / 18g pure vanilla extract

¼ cup / 57g whole milk

Sprinkles of choice

Yield: 9 by 13-inch cake

vanilla celebration cake, continued

The buttercream can be used immediately, or it can be covered tightly and refrigerated for 3–4 days. To use buttercream that has been refrigerated, let it come to room temperature. Give the buttercream a good stir with a sturdy spoon before using.

Once the cake has cooled, spread on the buttercream. I try to keep this fuss-free, swirling the buttercream into swoops and topping with sprinkles.

Covered, the cake can be stored at room temperature for up to 2 days. Wrapped and refrigerated, the cake will keep for up to 1 week.

cinnamon crumble cake

I'm not exaggerating when I say that this crumb cake will be the easiest crumb cake you'll ever make. And, possibly even better than its being easy, it's a cake I want to eat all the time. It makes a nice accompaniment to a cup of coffee or a spot of tea, and it's equally fantastic served with a dollop of yogurt and a bowl of fresh fruit.

solid gold

This recipe is pure Baking Gold. The components of the cake are some you're familiar with already. If you've made the Vanilla–Sour Cream Batter, then you know it's simple. And the crumble featured here is actually Brown Sugar–Oat Dough, which is as easy as melting butter and stirring a bowl of ingredients together. This crumble cake practically makes itself.

- 1 recipe Vanilla–Sour Cream Batter (page 118)

  2 tsp / 4g ground cinnamon

  2¼ cups / 450g Brown Sugar–Oat Dough (page 74), crumbled

Yield: 9 by 13-inch cake

Preheat the oven to 350°F. Line a 9 by 13-inch pan with parchment paper (see Element 5, page 4).

Pour the batter into the prepared pan and use a spatula to smooth it evenly into the corners.

Sprinkle on the cinnamon and use a fork or spoon to swirl it into the batter, swirling until all of it has been worked into the batter (there won't be any dry spots of cinnamon visible). Next, grab large pieces of Brown Sugar–Oat Dough, break them into smaller pieces, and plop them over the batter. Repeat until all the crumble is used and evenly distributed.

Bake the cake for 40–45 minutes, until the top is golden, springy to the touch, and a toothpick inserted into the center comes out clean. Let the cake cool in the pan for about 20 minutes, then cut and serve.

Wrapped, the cake can be stored at room temperature for up to 3 days. If you'd like, warm it for a few minutes in a 350°F oven.

citrus-vanilla cream-glazed blueberry cake

Dots of blueberries and a spark of citrus make this cake a real treat. Rather than pile this cake high with buttercream, you'll make a simple glaze with lemon juice and orange zest (flavors I love pairing with blueberry) and pour it over the cake. Flecks of zest, bits of vanilla, and the blue of blueberries peeking through—this cake is pretty and special all around. Speaking of special, this cake reminds me of garden parties and flowers and bright sun and delightful times. No, I have never eaten this cake at a garden party. In fact, I can't remember the last time I hosted or attended a garden party. That's how top-notch this cake is—it makes you think of things you've never even done!

solid gold

The glaze on this cake is Baking Gold because it works on lots of other baked items. I love it on cookies, muffins, quick breads, pound cake, and doughnuts, in addition to this cake. You'll wonder how you ever lived without it.

Preheat the oven to 350°F. Line a 9 by 13-inch pan with parchment paper (see Element 5, page 4).

Pour the batter into the prepared pan and use a spatula to smooth it evenly into the corners. Dot the top of the batter with the blueberries.

Bake the cake for 35–40 minutes, until it's golden, springy to the touch, and a toothpick inserted into the center comes out clean. Let the cake cool for about 30 minutes.

Make the glaze: Measure the powdered sugar into a large spouted cup or bowl. Add the lemon juice, cream, orange zest, and vanilla bean seeds. Stir until the glaze is smooth and pourable.

Pour the glaze over the cake and, using an offset spatula or a spoon, spread it all the way to the edges. Cut and serve.

This cake somehow tastes even better a day old. Covered, the cake can be stored at room temperature for up to 3 days.

- 1 recipe Vanilla–Sour Cream Batter (page 118)

1 cup / 115g frozen blueberries

Citrus-Vanilla Cream Glaze

2 cups / 227g powdered sugar, sifted

¼ cup / 64g freshly squeezed lemon juice

1 Tbsp / 15g heavy cream

1 Tbsp / 5g orange zest (from 1 medium orange)

1 vanilla bean pod, split and seeds scraped out

Yield: 9 by 13-inch cake

citrus-vanilla cream-glazed blueberry cake, continued

Baking Gold Reinventions

Blueberry Crumble Cake with Citrus-Vanilla Cream Glaze

Pour the batter into the pan and dot it with blueberries as directed. Crumble 2¼ cups / 450g Brown Sugar–Oat Dough (page 74) over the batter. Bake for 40–45 minutes, until the top is golden and a toothpick inserted into the center comes out clean. Make the glaze. When the cake has cooled for 10–15 minutes, use a skewer to poke 10 to 15 holes in the cake. Pour the glaze evenly over the top of the crumble, cut, and serve.

Blueberry-Orange Cake with Vanilla Bean–Cream Cheese Buttercream

Before pouring the batter into the pan, stir in 1 Tbsp / 5g orange zest (from 1 medium orange). Top with blueberries and bake as directed. Whip up 1 batch of Cream Cheese Buttercream (page 99), and at the end of mixing, add in the seeds from 1 split and scraped vanilla bean. Mix just until incorporated. Once the cake has cooled, cover it in a thick layer of buttercream, cut, and serve.

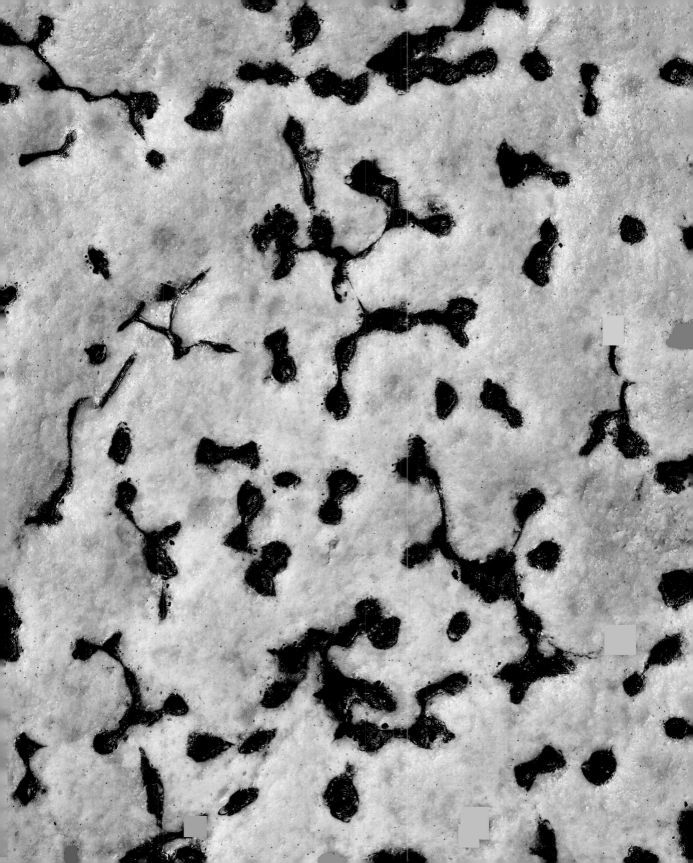

fun time surprise cake

Fun Time Surprise Cake is a fun time and a surprise because it features sprinkle buttercream—something I started making after a visit to a kindergarten class on Career Day. The kids I met that day were very fond of sprinkles—practically more fond of them than cake! They told me that one way to make cake better would be to add more sprinkles, and that's what I did. I like to use rainbow jimmies for this buttercream because they tend to hold on to their color better than other sprinkles. That said, if your sprinkles seep some rainbow colors into your buttercream, I would never (ever) consider that a bad thing!

solid gold

The key to this cake is to fight the urge to mix the chocolate chips into the batter. Instead, sprinkle the chocolate chips all over the top of the batter and leave them there to bake. The chips will stay chips, and the batter will pucker up and bake around them. That's what you want. If you'd like pale pink buttercream or some other shade, by all means, add 1 or 2 drops of color before you mix in the sprinkles. And, speaking of buttercream and sprinkles, you can top the buttercream with more sprinkles, mini chocolate chips, or even those chocolate candies that have white sprinkles on top (sometimes called nonpareils). Sno-Caps, which are miniature chocolate nonpareils, would be extra-cute.

Preheat the oven to 350°F. Line a 9 by 13-inch pan with parchment paper (see Element 5, page 4).

Pour the batter into the prepared pan and use a spatula to smooth it evenly into the corners. Sprinkle the chocolate chips evenly over the top of the batter.

Bake the cake for 35–40 minutes, until it's golden, springy to the touch, and a toothpick inserted into the center comes out clean. Allow the cake to cool completely.

1 recipe Vanilla–Sour Cream Batter (page 118)

1½ cups / 9 oz / 255g chocolate chips

1 recipe Cream Cheese Buttercream (page 99)

1 cup / 170g rainbow sprinkles (also sold as rainbow jimmies), plus more for finishing

Mini chocolate chips for finishing (optional)

Sno-Caps or other chocolate nonpareils for finishing (optional)

Yield: 9 by 13-inch cake or 12 (2¾-inch) round pieces

continued →

fun time surprise cake, continued

Place the buttercream in a large bowl. Pour the sprinkles over the buttercream. Gently fold the sprinkles into the buttercream.

Spread a thick layer of the buttercream over the cake. Decorate the cake with your choice of additional sprinkles, mini chocolate chips, or (my favorite) Sno-Caps. When I'm feeling a little fancy, I like to cut this cake into round pieces before covering it with buttercream, sprinkles, and candy. To make it easy, I lift the whole cake out of the pan and place it on a cutting board. Then use a 2¾-inch round cutter to cut it into 12 round pieces. Once cut, I pipe or spread on buttercream and top with sprinkles and candy. For more easy "fancy" cake ideas, see page 120.

Covered, the cake can be stored at room temperature for 1 day. Wrapped and refrigerated, the cake can keep for up to 1 week, although it's most enjoyable to eat at room temperature.

strawberry and butterscotch whipped cream cake

I love a layer of whipped cream, especially if it's on a cake. And I also love a layer of whipped cream on fruit. This concoction has both: Whipped cream on cake and fruit. What a dream! And remember, it doesn't have to be strawberry season to enjoy this cake. In January, use high-quality frozen berries and it will feel like summer.

solid gold

Yes, this cake is made up of three parts, and yes, all three are easy to make. Even easier, you can bake the cake a day in advance, and when you're ready to serve it, simply add the strawberries and whipped cream and you'll have a fancy cake in no time. I've made this cake as individual squares that I top with berries and cream right before serving, and you might like to do the same. See below for tips on how to do it.

Preheat the oven to 350°F. Line a 9 by 13-inch pan with parchment paper (see Element 5, page 4).

Pour the batter into the prepared pan and use a spatula to smooth it evenly into the corners. Bake the cake for 35–40 minutes, until it's golden, springy to the touch, and a toothpick inserted into the center comes out clean. Allow the cake to cool completely.

Make the Butterscotch Whipped Cream: Chill a bowl and a whisk. Pour the cream into the bowl and add the brown sugar and vanilla. Whisk the cream until stiff-ish peaks form. Take care that you don't turn it into butter by overwhipping. Use immediately. (Yes, you can use a mixer with the whisk attachment to whip the cream!)

When you're ready to serve the cake, spoon the Strawberry Compote over it. Top the compote with the Butterscotch Whipped Cream, using the back of a spoon to give it some pretty swirls. Alternatively, use the parchment paper to lift

1 recipe Vanilla–Sour Cream Batter (page 118)

Butterscotch Whipped Cream

2 cups / 480g heavy cream

⅓ cup / 72g brown sugar

2 tsp / 12g pure vanilla extract

1 recipe Strawberry Compote (page 66), cold

Yield: 9 by 13-inch cake

continued →

strawberry and butterscotch whipped cream cake, continued

the cooled cake out of the pan. Cut the cake into 12 equal pieces. Spoon some Strawberry Compote over each piece. Top with a generous dollop of Butterscotch Whipped Cream.

Plan to enjoy this cake the day you assemble it. That said, if you cover and refrigerate it, it will not disappoint the next day or the day after that. Especially for breakfast.

Baking Gold Reinvention

Peach and Butterscotch Whipped Cream Cake

Use an equal amount of peaches instead of strawberries in the Strawberry Compote from page 66. Bake the cake and whip up the Butterscotch Whipped Cream as directed. When the cake has cooled, spoon the peach compote over it. Top the cake with the Butterscotch Whipped Cream, cut, and serve.

crunchy, creamy coconut cake

Hello, I'd like to introduce you to your new favorite combination of flavors all wrapped up in a big cake. Vanilla. Toffee. Buttercream. Toasted coconut. Maybe this cake will become your new special-occasion cake. Put it on your invite list because this cake definitely loves a party. (Pictured on page 141.)

solid gold

I love mixing toffee into cakes and cookies. It bakes into something crunchy and buttery—a sensation that is hard to resist, especially in this cake. (Warning: You're going to want to eat the entire top off of this cake when it comes out of the oven. And I am most definitely speaking from experience here.)

Preheat the oven to 350°F. Line a 9 by 13-inch pan with parchment paper (see Element 5, page 4).

Pour the batter into the prepared pan and use a spatula to smooth it evenly into the corners. Sprinkle the toffee bits over the top. You don't need to stir them in or encourage them to sink.

Bake the cake for 35–40 minutes, until it's golden, springy to the touch, and a toothpick inserted into the center comes out clean. Let the cake cool completely.

Spread a lovely thick layer of the buttercream over the top of the cake. Shower the toasted coconut evenly over the buttercream. Cut and serve.

Covered, the cake can be stored at cool room temperature for 1 day. Wrapped and refrigerated, the cake will keep for at least 3 days, although it's most enjoyable to eat at room temperature.

Baking Gold Reinvention

Toffee Fudge Cake

Bake the cake as directed with the toffee baked into the batter. Pour barely warm Cocoa Fudge Sauce (page 103) over the top of the cooled cake instead of Cream Cheese Buttercream and coconut.

1 recipe Vanilla–Sour Cream Batter (page 118)

¾ cup / 120g toffee bits (plain toffee, sometimes called Bits o' Brickle, not chocolate-coated; see page 79)

1 recipe Cream Cheese Buttercream (page 99)

1½ cups / 130g sweetened, shredded coconut, toasted (see page 22)

Yield: 9 by 13-inch cake

crunchy, creamy coconut cake

1 Magic Mix

Oh, cookies. How I love cookies. I love making them, scooping them, baking them, and eating them. I feel complete when my freezer is stocked with a few dozen cookies waiting to be settled into the oven and baked. And brownies? There has never been a brownie that I would turn down. All that chocolate and all those possibilities for flavor? Brownies and cookies all the way.

With a bin of Baking Gold Mix in your pantry, you're ready to make cookies and brownies anytime.

The wild side of me loves the crazy crunch of pretzels in the Pretzel-Toffee-Chocolate-Cherry Cookies (page 153). And the fancy cookie devotee in me loves the spark of orange in the Ginger-Molasses Cookies with Orange Zest (page 157). And remember: Slightly overbaked cookies will produce a far superior cookie-eating experience than will underbaking, so make sure those edges are golden.

What makes Baking Gold Mix pure gold? The fact that if you have a container of it in your pantry, you are ready to bake cookies and brownies *without planning ahead*. I try to never be without it.

baking gold mix

Baking Gold Mix is a single dry mix that works as the base for loads of different cookie and brownie recipes, all of which can be made on a moment's notice when you have the mix on hand. It doesn't sound possible, right? Well, it is. Behold the magic.

solid gold

A large airtight container or gallon-size resealable bags are perfect for storing the mix. The recipe yields enough mix for about 4 batches of cookies or brownies, and you can store it in your pantry as easily as you do flour. (See Element 6, page 5, for more about pantry storage.) If you think the recipe is too big for you (it's not), you can always halve the ingredients for a 6-cup / 742g yield.

Place the flour, baking soda, and salt in a large bowl and whisk to combine. Whisk again to make doubly sure the baking soda and salt are evenly distributed. Transfer to an airtight container and store in a cool, dry place for up to 3 months. Always whisk before using.

12 cups / 1.44kg all-purpose flour

1 Tbsp plus 1 tsp / 24g baking soda

4 tsp / 20g kosher salt

Yield: Approximately 12 cups / 1.48kg

bits of chocolate and sea salt cookies

Yes, you can use any chocolate you'd like in these cookies. That said, I really love a mix of bittersweet chocolate and slightly milkier chocolate. If we're getting chocolate-specific, I'd say the bittersweet chocolate could be in the neighborhood of 70% cacao and the milkier chocolate could come in between 45 and 50%. If you like the idea of salt on cookies, you'll love these with a sprinkle of sea salt flakes on top. Simply sprinkle it on right after baking.

solid gold

A not-so-secret ingredient in my cookies? It's chopped chocolate, of course! I like to skip the chips and instead buy chunks of chocolate that I chop myself. When you bite into a cookie made with chopped chocolate, you see multiple layers of chocolate throughout the cookie, and it's that layering that I love. When chopping chocolate, you'll have some dusty, flaky bits and pieces of chocolate left behind on your cutting board— add those to your dough! They turn into chocolate freckles in every bite. Big hint: Even if you chop only half of the chocolate that's called for in a recipe (and use chips for the rest), your dough will have some fantastic freckly layers.

Preheat the oven to 350°F. Line two sheet pans with parchment paper.

Place the butter and sugars in the bowl of a stand mixer fitted with the paddle attachment. Beat on medium speed for 2–3 minutes. Scrape the bottom and sides of the bowl to help you get a look at what's going on inside. If you see any streaks or specks of butter, run the mixer a little longer.

Add the eggs, one at a time, fully incorporating the first egg before adding the second. Add the vanilla and continue mixing until the eggs have been incorporated and the mixture is beginning to look like dough, 2–3 minutes. Scrape the bowl again, making sure all of the eggs have been mixed in evenly. If you see unmixed egg, run the mixer a little longer.

1 cup / 226g unsalted butter, at cool room temperature (see page 151)

1 cup / 215g brown sugar

½ cup / 100g granulated sugar

2 large eggs

2 tsp / 12g pure vanilla extract

3 cups plus 2 Tbsp / 380g Baking Gold Mix (page 146)

3 cups / 18 oz / 510g chocolate, chopped

Sea salt flakes for finishing (optional)

Yield: Approximately 36 cookies

continued →

bits of chocolate and sea salt cookies, continued

Add the Baking Gold Mix and run the mixer until it is fully incorporated. Add the chocolate and run the mixer until it is evenly dispersed throughout.

Using a 2 Tbsp / 30ml scoop, portion the dough onto the prepared sheet pans, placing 8 cookies per pan (see opposite). Bake for 13–15 minutes, until the edges of the cookies are golden and the centers no longer look wet. Repeat until all of the cookies have been baked, or refrigerate or freeze a portion of the scooped dough for later.

To refrigerate, wrap the sheet pan tightly and refrigerate the dough for up to 3 days. Bake the cookies directly from the refrigerator, adding 2–3 minutes to the baking time.

To freeze, refrigerate the sheet pan of scooped dough (uncovered is fine) until the cookies are firm, about 30 minutes. Transfer the scoops of dough to a freezer-safe resealable bag, remembering to label it with what's inside (see Element 3, page 4). Freeze the bag of scooped dough for up to 3 months. When ready to bake, remove as many cookies as you'd like from the bag, arranging them 8 to a prepared sheet pan. Bake without thawing, adding about 5 minutes to the baking time.

Once the cookies have been baked, sprinkle the sea salt over them and let cool on the pans.

Store the cookies in your cookie jar (or other storage container) for up to 3 days.

Cool Room Temperature

When creaming butter for cookies, I like to use butter that's at cool room temperature. I'm not talking butter that has been sitting on a counter in a hot house on a 90°F day. I'm talking butter that's relaxing on a cool afternoon at about 68°F. To me, that's cool room temperature butter.

Baking Gold Reinvention

Chocolate-Pecan-Toffee Cookies

Reduce the chocolate to 2 cups / 340g. Add 1 cup / 100g chopped toasted pecans and ½ cup / 100g toffee bits to the dough along with the chocolate.

8 to a pan

When baking cookies on sheet pans, I have a rule: 8 cookies per pan and no more. This allows the cookies to bake evenly, without the risk of their oozing into one another. Starting at one end of the pan, place 2 cookies, then 1 cookie, 2 cookies, then 1 cookie, then finish with 2 cookies, all equally spaced in a hopscotch pattern.

pretzel-toffee-chocolate-cherry cookies

Buttery toffee, salty pretzels, sweet (or sour!) cherries—plus chocolate? Sometimes crunchy, sometimes chewy, and always unexpected, these cookies are an adventure in flavor and texture—each bite a little different and never the same bite twice. You'll wonder why you never put pretzels in cookies before.

solid gold

Don't worry about having a specific brown sugar in your pantry for these cookies—light and dark are interchangeable here (see Element 7, page 5). If you only have pretzel sticks (and not twists), by all means, use them (please be sure they are not unsalted!). As for chocolate, go with what you like. Dark chocolate is nicely balanced by dried sweet cherries, and a milkier chocolate is nice with dried sour cherries. It's up to you—these are your cookies.

Preheat the oven to 350°F. Line two sheet pans with parchment paper.

Place the butter in the bowl of a stand mixer fitted with the paddle attachment. Beat on medium speed until it's very smooth, 2–3 minutes. Add the brown sugar and granulated sugar and beat again on medium for 2–3 minutes, until pale in color and fluffy in volume. Scrape the bottom and sides of the bowl.

Add the eggs, one at a time, fully incorporating the first egg before adding the second. Add the vanilla with the second egg and mix until it starts to look more like a dough, about 1 minute.

Add the Baking Gold Mix and mix on low until you no longer see traces of it. Scrape the bowl again and add the chocolate, pretzels, toffee, and cherries, mixing to incorporate.

Using a 2 Tbsp / 30ml scoop, portion the dough onto the prepared sheet pans, placing 8 cookies per pan (see page 151). Bake for 16–18 minutes, until the tops are no longer shiny and the edges of all the cookies are golden. Repeat until all of the

1 cup / 226g unsalted butter, at cool room temperature (see page 151)

1 cup / 215g brown sugar

⅔ cup / 135g granulated sugar

2 large eggs

1 Tbsp / 18g pure vanilla extract

3 cups / 360g Baking Gold Mix (page 146)

⅔ cup / 4 oz / 113g chocolate, either chopped or chips

½ cup / 100g toffee bits (plain toffee, sometimes called Bits o' Brickle, not chocolate coated; see page 79)

1¾ cups / 75g broken pretzel twists

½ cup / 75g dried sweet or sour cherries

Yield: Approximately 36 cookies

continued →

cookies have been baked, or refrigerate or freeze a portion of the scooped dough for later.

To refrigerate, wrap the sheet pan tightly and refrigerate the dough for up to 3 days. Bake the cookies directly from the refrigerator, adding 2–3 minutes to the baking time.

To freeze, refrigerate the sheet pan of scooped dough (uncovered is fine) until the cookies are firm, about 30 minutes. Transfer the scoops of dough to a freezer-safe resealable bag, remembering to label it with what's inside (see Element 3, page 4). Freeze the bag of scooped dough for up to 3 months. When ready to bake, remove as many cookies as you'd like from the bag, arranging them 8 to a prepared sheet pan. Bake without thawing, adding about 5 minutes to the baking time.

Let the cookies cool on the pans. Store the cookies in your cookie jar (or other storage container) for up to 3 days.

Baking Gold Reinvention

Toffee-Chocolate Cookies

Omit the pretzels and cherries. Increase the chocolate to 1¼ cups / 213g and the toffee to ¾ cup / 175g. Proceed as directed in the recipe.

The Scoop on Scoops

Every cookie made with Baking Gold Mix is scooped with a 2 Tbsp / 30ml scoop. As a result, the cookies are neither too big nor too small; they're generous without being overwhelming. To get uniform balls of dough scoop after scoop, dig into the dough with your scoop and pull it to the side of your bowl while pressing it against the bowl and pulling upward. This motion will pack the scoop with the dough. Once you get to the top of the bowl, odds are your scoop will have a little brim of excess dough around the edge—wipe that brim away, leaving the excess dough in the mixer bowl.

ginger-molasses cookies with orange zest

I know what you're thinking. You're eyeballing this list of ingredients, trying to decide what you can leave out. You see that orange zest and you think, "Who needs it? I'm going to skip it." That's fine. I get it. Yet, allow me to tell you a little secret: The orange zest takes these cookies from a good cookie to a crave-worthy cookie.

solid gold

In this recipe, Baking Gold Mix is transformed by the addition of ginger cookie spices. Molasses gives the finished cookies a deep, rich flavor that's made even better with the accent of orange zest. Next time you're at the grocery, stop by the baking aisle and pick up a jar of molasses. It'll keep in your cool pantry for a long while (and you'll certainly be making these cookies more than once).

Preheat the oven to 350°F. Line two sheet pans with parchment paper.

Combine the butter and sugars in the bowl of a stand mixer fitted with the paddle attachment. Mix on medium speed until the mixture is pale in color and fluffy in volume. This will take 4–5 minutes.

In a small bowl, stir together the molasses, egg, and orange zest. Add this to the mixer bowl and mix on low. The contents of the mixer bowl will go from looking separated and shiny to looking more dough-like.

Place the Baking Gold Mix in a bowl. Add the ginger, cinnamon, cloves, and black pepper and whisk to combine. Add the dry ingredients to the mixer bowl and mix on low until you no longer see traces of it. Cover and chill the dough until it is firm enough to hold its shape when scooped, 20–30 minutes.

Place the granulated sugar for coating in a bowl. Using a 2 Tbsp / 30ml scoop to portion the dough, drop the

¾ cup / 170g unsalted butter, at cool room temperature (see page 151)

¾ cup / 162g brown sugar

¼ cup / 50g granulated sugar, plus more for coating

3 Tbsp / 65g unsulphured molasses

1 large egg

Grated zest of 1 orange

2⅓ cups / 280g Baking Gold Mix (page 146)

1 tsp / 2g ground ginger

½ tsp / 1g ground cinnamon

½ tsp / 1g ground cloves

¼ tsp / 1g black pepper

Yield: Approximately 20 cookies

continued →

ginger-molasses cookies with orange zest, continued

scooped dough into the bowl of sugar and roll around to coat evenly. Place the sugared scoops of dough on the prepared sheet pans, placing 8 cookies per pan (see page 151). Bake for 14–16 minutes, until the edges of the cookies are firm and the centers are still soft. Repeat until all of the cookies have been baked, or refrigerate or freeze a portion of the scooped dough for later.

To refrigerate, wrap the sheet pan tightly and refrigerate the dough for up to 3 days. Bake the cookies directly from the refrigerator, adding 2–3 minutes to the baking time.

To freeze, refrigerate the sheet pan of scooped dough (uncovered is fine) until the cookies are firm, about 30 minutes. Transfer the scoops of dough to a freezer-safe resealable bag, remembering to label it with what's inside (see Element 3, page 4). Freeze the bag of scooped dough for up to 3 months. When ready to bake, remove as many cookies as you'd like from the bag, arranging them 8 to a prepared sheet pan. Bake without thawing, adding about 5 minutes to the baking time.

Let the cookies cool on the pans. Store the cookies in your cookie jar (or other storage container) for up to 3 days.

berry-cardamom cookies with toasted walnuts

I love these cookies because of the oats. And the blueberries. And the walnuts. These cookies are practically a bowl of oatmeal (something I tell myself when I want cookies for breakfast). Could these cookies work with cherries and almonds in place of the blueberries and walnuts? Definitely. What about raisins and salty smoked nuts? Yes! To make the change, simply swap the blueberries and walnuts called for in the recipe with 1 cup each of the dried fruit and nuts of your choice.

solid gold

If you're following the Elements of Baking Gold (Element 8 in particular, page 5) and have some pre-toasted nuts on hand, use them here. If not, toast enough walnuts for this recipe plus a bit more so they're ready for next time. I use cinnamon, cardamom, and nutmeg in this recipe, although you could easily substitute an equal amount of other baking spices if that's what you have in your spice drawer. Yes, the cardamom gives these cookies a special edge. Still, use what you have and don't worry too much—they're cookies after all!

Preheat the oven to 350°F. Line two sheet pans with parchment paper.

Combine the butter and sugars in the bowl of a stand mixer fitted with the paddle attachment. Beat on medium speed for 4 minutes, or until light in color and fluffy in volume. Use a spatula to scrape the bowl, making sure all the butter is incorporated.

Combine the eggs and vanilla in a bowl. Add this to the mixer bowl in three additions, fully incorporating each addition before adding the next. Continue to mix until the contents of the bowl start to smooth out. Scrape the bottom and sides of the bowl.

¾ cup / 170g unsalted butter, at cool room temperature (see page 151)

1 cup / 215g brown sugar

1 cup / 200g granulated sugar

2 large eggs

1 Tbsp / 18g pure vanilla extract

3 cups / 300g rolled oats

1½ cups / 180g Baking Gold Mix (page 146)

½ tsp / 1g ground cinnamon

½ tsp / 1g ground cardamom

½ tsp / 1g ground nutmeg

1 cup / 160g dried blueberries

1 cup / 100g walnut pieces, toasted (see page 21)

Yield: Approximately 36 cookies

continued →

berry-cardamom cookies
with toasted walnuts, continued

In a large bowl, stir together the oats and Baking Gold Mix. Add the cinnamon, cardamom, and nutmeg and stir to incorporate. Add this mixture to the mixer bowl and mix on low until you no longer see traces of it. Add the blueberries and walnuts and continue to mix on low until the nuts and berries are incorporated.

Using a 2 Tbsp / 30ml scoop, portion the dough onto the prepared sheet pans, placing 8 cookies per pan (see page 151). Bake for 14–16 minutes, until the cookies are nicely bronzed and set. The cookies should not be gooey in the center. Repeat until all of the cookies are baked, or refrigerate or freeze a portion of the scooped dough for later.

To refrigerate, wrap the sheet pan tightly and refrigerate the dough for up to 3 days. Bake the cookies directly from the refrigerator, adding 2–3 minutes to the baking time.

To freeze, refrigerate the sheet pan of scooped dough (uncovered is fine) until the cookies are firm, about 30 minutes. Transfer the scoops of dough to a freezer-safe resealable bag, remembering to label it with what's inside (see Element 3, page 4). Freeze the bag of scooped dough for up to 3 months. When ready to bake, remove as many cookies as you'd like from the bag, arranging them 8 to a prepared sheet pan. Bake directly from the freezer, adding about 5 minutes to the baking time.

Let the cookies cool on the pans. Store the cookies in your cookie jar (or other storage container) for up to 3 days.

peanut butter-chocolate cookies

These cookies are very peanut-buttery. You'll love them with a glass of milk after a long day at school, work, wherever your day takes you. These are the ideal cookie jar cookies—they seem to improve for at least three days after baking.

solid gold

Natural peanut butter (made with only peanuts and salt) works nicely here because there's plenty of sugar in the recipe. If you only have sweetened peanut butter, you can certainly use it. Simply expect a sweeter cookie. You can play around with this recipe—eliminate the chocolate and you have a great peanut butter cookie. Or you could add more stuff: Mix in up to ½ cup / 85g total salted peanuts, chopped peanut butter cups, or white chocolate chips in addition to the chocolate called for in the recipe. I, of course, vote for this second option.

Preheat the oven to 350°F. Line two sheet pans with parchment paper.

Combine the butter and sugars in the bowl of a stand mixer fitted with the paddle attachment. Gradually increase the speed of the mixer to medium and cream the butter and sugars until light in color and fluffy in volume, about 5 minutes.

Scrape the bowl. With the mixer running on low, add the eggs and vanilla. Continue to mix until the contents of the bowl smooth out.

Add the peanut butter and mix for 2 minutes, or until smooth. Scrape the bowl again to make sure all of the peanut butter is mixed in.

Add the Baking Gold Mix to the bowl and run the mixer until you no longer see traces of it. Add the chocolate and mix on low just until incorporated. Cover the dough and refrigerate until it's firm enough to scoop, 20–30 minutes.

Place the granulated sugar for coating in a bowl. Using a 2 Tbsp / 30ml scoop to portion the dough, drop the scooped

1 cup / 226g unsalted butter, at cool room temperature (see page 151)

1 cup / 215g brown sugar

1 cup / 200g granulated sugar, plus more for coating

2 large eggs

2 tsp / 12g pure vanilla extract

1⅔ cups / 454g peanut butter

3¼ cups / 390g Baking Gold Mix (page 146)

2 cups / 12 oz / 340g chocolate chunks or chocolate chips

Yield: Approximately 48 cookies

continued →

peanut butter-chocolate cookies, continued

dough into the bowl of sugar and roll around to coat evenly. Place the sugared scoops of dough on the prepared sheet pans, placing 8 cookies per pan (see page 151). Using the tines of a fork, press a crosshatch pattern into the top of each cookie, flattening them into puck-like shapes. Bake for 13–15 minutes, until the edges are set and the cookies are pale and barely golden at the edges. Repeat until all of the cookies are baked, or refrigerate or freeze a portion of the scooped dough for later.

To refrigerate, wrap the sheet pan tightly and refrigerate the dough for up to 3 days. Bake the cookies directly from the refrigerator, adding 2–3 minutes to the baking time.

To freeze, refrigerate the sheet pan of scooped dough (uncovered is fine) until the cookies are firm, about 30 minutes. Transfer the scoops of dough to a freezer-safe resealable bag, remembering to label it with what's inside (see Element 3, page 4). Freeze the bag of scooped dough for up to 3 months. When ready to bake, remove as many cookies as you'd like from the bag, arranging them 8 to a prepared sheet pan. Bake directly from the freezer, adding about 5 minutes to the baking time.

Let the cookies cool on the pans. Store the cookies in your cookie jar (or other storage container) for up to 3 days.

Baking Gold Reinvention

Peanut Butter Cookies

Omit the chocolate and proceed as directed.

chocolate-chocolate-chocolate cookies

Whether warm from the oven or plucked from the depths of your cookie jar, these cookies are bursting with chocolate (three types!) and are definitely meant to be paired with a glass of cold milk.

solid gold

The magic in these cookies is the cocoa powder. It takes only a small amount to add rich, chocolatey goodness to the dough, which is then complemented by the addition of white and dark (or milk!) chocolate chips. (And, yes, I use chips in these cookies because I love the bite of the solid chips of chocolate mixed in with soft, chocolatey dough.) I've found that I especially love these cookies when I make them with dark brown sugar. If you have it, use it.

Preheat the oven to 350°F. Line two sheet pans with parchment paper.

Combine the butter and sugars in the bowl of a stand mixer fitted with the paddle attachment. Beat on medium speed for 5 minutes. Scrape the bottom and sides of the mixer bowl. If you see any specks of unmixed butter, run the mixer a little bit longer.

Add the eggs, one at a time, fully incorporating the first egg before adding the second. Add the vanilla with the second egg and mix for about 1 minute, until the contents of the bowl start to resemble a dough. Scrape the bowl again.

Place the Baking Gold Mix in a large bowl and add the cocoa powder, stirring to combine. Add to the mixer bowl and mix on low until you no longer see traces of the dry ingredients.

Add all of the chocolate chips and mix on low until they're evenly dotting the dough.

Using a 2 Tbsp / 30ml scoop, portion the dough onto the prepared sheet pans, placing 8 cookies per pan (see page 151). Bake for 14–16 minutes, until the edges of the cookies are firm

1 cup / 226g unsalted butter, at cool room temperature (see page 151)

⅔ cup / 135g granulated sugar

⅔ cup / 145g dark brown sugar

2 large eggs

1 Tbsp / 18g pure vanilla extract

2⅔ cups / 325g Baking Gold Mix (page 146)

¼ cup / 25g cocoa powder

1 cup / 6 oz / 170g dark or milk chocolate chips

1 cup / 6 oz / 170g white chocolate chips

Yield: Approximately 30 cookies

continued →

and the centers are still soft. Repeat until all of the cookies are baked, or refrigerate or freeze a portion of the scooped dough for later.

To refrigerate, wrap the sheet pan tightly and refrigerate the dough for up to 3 days. Bake the cookies directly from the refrigerator, adding 2–3 minutes to the baking time.

To freeze, refrigerate the sheet pan of scooped dough (uncovered is fine) until the cookies are firm, about 30 minutes. Transfer the scoops of dough to a freezer-safe resealable bag, remembering to label it with what's inside (see Element 3, page 4). Freeze the bag of scooped dough for up to 3 months. When ready to bake, remove as many cookies as you'd like from the bag, arranging them 8 to a prepared sheet pan. Bake directly from the freezer, adding about 5 minutes to the baking time.

Let the cookies cool on the pans. Store the cookies in your cookie jar (or other storage container) for up to 3 days.

Baking Gold Reinvention

Chocolate-Chocolate-Peanut Butter Cookies

Forget about the white chocolate chips and replace them with peanut butter chips. Mix and bake as directed.

malted milk-white chocolate brownies

These rich and amazingly dense brownies are deep in flavor thanks to malted milk powder. It makes them creamy, toasty, and a little mysterious. Not as malty as a chocolate malt, and absolutely not a plain brownie (hello, white chocolate), these are the brownies to call on when you're looking for a departure from the ordinary.

solid gold

Malted milk powder is a secret bakery ingredient. Bakers sneak it into cookies, cakes, muffins, and even bread. It brings a surprising amount of flavor to almost everything it touches. With that in mind, these brownies are creamier and richer due to the addition of malted milk powder. You can find it in your regular grocery store, and some stores even carry malted milk powder in bulk! If you're lucky enough to have a store that does, get this powder in bulk and store it in your cool pantry.

¾ cup / 170g unsalted butter

2 cups / 400g granulated sugar

1 cup / 100g cocoa powder

½ cup / 70g malted milk powder

1 Tbsp / 18g pure vanilla extract

3 large eggs, cracked into a bowl and stirred with a fork

1 cup / 120g Baking Gold Mix (page 146)

¾ cup / 4½ oz / 128g white chocolate chips

Yield: 12 large or 24 small brownies

Preheat the oven to 350°F. Line a 9 by 13-inch pan with parchment paper (see Element 5, page 4).

In a medium saucepan, melt the butter over medium heat. In a bowl, combine the sugar, cocoa powder, and malt powder. Once the butter has melted, add the sugar, cocoa powder, malt powder, and vanilla to the butter and stir. Keep the pan on the heat for about 2 minutes, stirring continuously. The mixture will look granulated. Remove the pan from the heat. Add the eggs, stirring until they are fully incorporated and the mixture looks smooth and glossy. Add the Baking Gold Mix and stir until you no longer see traces of it. Let the batter cool for 5 minutes, stirring occasionally. Mix in the white chocolate chips. The batter will be very thick.

Tip the saucepan and ease the batter into the prepared pan, spreading it to the corners. Bake for 32–35 minutes, until the edges are firm and the center is set.

Cool completely. Cut into pieces (see Element 1, page 7).

Wrapped, the brownies will keep at room temperature for about 4 days.

fruit and nut brownies

Fudgy and not even close to cakey, these are my very favorite version of brownies. There's a ton of room for variation here. The cherries can be replaced by any dried fruit you like. If you'd rather use chopped smoked almonds or toasted hazelnuts in place of toasted pecans, do it. And if you'd like to use a combination of dark and milk chocolates, that sounds smart to me, too.

solid gold

Following Element 11 (see page 7), these brownies can be cut into any size. Don't get fussy! If you'd like a few big brownies alongside some not-so-big ones, I support that decision. This batter (and all the brownie batters that follow) can be prepared a day ahead. Simply pour the batter into the prepared pan, wrap, and refrigerate. When you're ready, unwrap the brownies and bake, adding about 5 minutes to the baking time.

Preheat the oven to 350°F. Line a 9 by 13-inch pan with parchment paper (see Element 5, page 4).

In a large saucepan, melt the butter over medium heat. In a medium bowl, combine the sugar and cocoa powder. Once the butter has melted, add the sugar, cocoa powder, and vanilla to the butter and stir. Keep the pan on the heat for about 2 minutes, stirring continuously. The mixture will look granulated. Remove the pan from the heat. Add the eggs, stirring until they are fully incorporated and the mixture looks smooth and glossy. Add the Baking Gold Mix and stir until you no longer see traces of it. Let the batter cool for 5 minutes, stirring occasionally. Mix in the cherries, pecans, toffee, and chocolate. The batter will be very thick.

Tip the saucepan and ease the batter into the prepared pan, spreading it to the corners. Bake for 32–35 minutes, until the edges are firm and the center is set.

continued →

¾ cup / 170g unsalted butter

2 cups / 400g granulated sugar

1 cup / 100g cocoa powder

1 Tbsp / 18g pure vanilla extract

3 large eggs, cracked into a bowl and stirred with a fork

1 cup / 120g Baking Gold Mix (page 146)

½ cup / 75g dried cherries or raisins

½ cup / 50g pecan pieces, toasted (see page 21)

¼ cup / 50g toffee bits (plain toffee, sometimes called Bits o' Brickle; see page 79)

¾ cup / 4½ oz / 128g chocolate chips or chopped chocolate

Yield: 12 large or 24 small brownies

fruit and nut brownies, continued

Cool completely. Cut into pieces (see Element 11, page 7).

Wrapped, the brownies will keep at room temperature for about 4 days.

Brownie Parchment

Here's an easy way to remove the parchment paper from the bottom of your brownies: Remove the brownies from the pan by grabbing the edges of the parchment paper and lifting the brownies up and out. Next, use the parchment to help you flip the slab of brownies over so that you can peel the paper off the bottom. Once the parchment has been removed, use a spatula to help you flip the slab back over onto a cutting board.

double vanilla-spice brownies

What can be said about brownies that hasn't been said a million times before? They're chocolatey, they're rich, and you can mix anything you'd like into them. These brownies are made with extra vanilla, cinnamon, and ancho chile. Maybe they're the exception to the "million times before" rule?

solid gold

Double vanilla makes these brownies doubly delicious. And for the chocolate pieces that get pressed into the batter before baking? I recommend dark chocolate here. It's the perfect match for the super-vanilla batter warmed up with cinnamon and chile.

Preheat the oven to 350°F. Line a 9 by 13-inch pan with parchment paper (see Element 5, page 4).

In a large saucepan, melt the butter over medium heat. In a medium bowl, combine the sugar and cocoa powder. Once the butter has melted, add the sugar, cocoa powder, and vanilla to the butter and stir. Keep the pan on the heat for about 2 minutes, stirring continuously. The mixture will look granulated. Remove the pan from the heat. Add the eggs, stirring until they are fully incorporated and the mixture looks smooth and glossy.

In another medium bowl, combine the Baking Gold Mix, cinnamon, and chile powder. Add this mixture to the saucepan and stir until you no longer see traces of it. Let the batter cool for 5 minutes, stirring occasionally. The batter will be very thick.

Tip the saucepan and ease the batter into the prepared pan, spreading it to the corners. Sprinkle the chocolate over the top of the batter and press the pieces into the batter to help them sink. Bake for 32–35 minutes, until the edges are firm and the center is set.

Cool completely. Cut into pieces (see Element 11, page 7).

Wrapped, the brownies will keep at room temperature for about 4 days.

¾ cup / 170g unsalted butter

2 cups / 400g granulated sugar

1 cup / 100g cocoa powder

2 Tbsp / 36g pure vanilla extract

3 large eggs, cracked into a bowl and stirred with a fork

1 cup / 120g Baking Gold Mix (page 146)

½ tsp / 1g ground cinnamon

½ tsp / 1g ancho chile powder

1 cup / 6 oz / 170g dark chocolate chips or chopped chocolate

Yield: 12 large or 24 small brownies

caramelized milk brownies

These brownies are not for the casual treat eater. They are for the serious enthusiast who rarely meets a baked delight that is too rich or too sweet. Don't skip stirring in the chocolate pieces at the end—they create little pockets of chocolate, and those pockets are my favorite part of this brownie experience.

solid gold

Yes, you're caramelizing sweetened condensed milk here, much like in the recipe for the apricot tarts on page 87. This technique results in a caramel that, when warm, can be poured over the top of pie, cheesecake, ice cream, and fruit crisps. It makes a terrific sandwich cookie filling, too. What I like most about caramelizing a can of sweetened condensed milk is that it's nearly hands-off yet produces a caramelly concoction that tastes like I spent all day making it.

Make the Caramelized Milk: Pour the can of sweetened condensed milk into the top of a double boiler or a heatproof bowl set over (but not touching) a pan of simmering water. Increase the heat to high and bring the water in the bottom of the double boiler to a vigorous boil, then immediately turn the dial to the high side of medium. Cover the top of the double boiler and allow the sweetened condensed milk to cook until caramelized, stirring every 30 minutes or so, for about 90 minutes total. Check the water level when you stir and add more as needed. When finished, the sweetened condensed milk will be thick and a golden caramel color. Stir in the salt. Turn off the heat and leave the double boiler in place for 10 minutes. The caramel is now ready to use.

The sauce can be made ahead, stored in the refrigerator, and gently rewarmed when you're ready to use it.

Preheat the oven to 350°F. Line a 9 by 13-inch pan with parchment paper (see Element 5, page 4).

Caramelized Milk

14 oz / 396g can sweetened condensed milk

1 tsp / 5g kosher salt

¾ cup / 170g unsalted butter

2 cups / 400g granulated sugar

1 cup / 100g cocoa powder

1 Tbsp / 18g pure vanilla extract

3 large eggs, cracked into a bowl and stirred with a fork

1 cup / 120g Baking Gold Mix (page 146)

6 oz / 170g chocolate, chopped or broken into pieces (1 cup)

Yield: 12 large or 24 small brownies

continued →

caramelized milk brownies, continued

In a large saucepan, melt the butter over medium heat. In a bowl, combine the sugar and cocoa powder. Once the butter has melted, add the sugar, cocoa powder, and vanilla to the butter and stir. Keep the pan on the heat for about 2 minutes, stirring continuously. The mixture will look granulated. Remove the pan from the heat. Add the eggs, stirring until they are fully incorporated and the mixture looks smooth and glossy. Add the Baking Gold Mix and stir until you no longer see traces of it. Let the batter cool for five minutes, stirring occasionally, then mix in the chocolate pieces. The batter will be very thick.

Tip the saucepan and ease the batter into the parchment-lined pan, spreading it to the corners of the pan. Spoon the Caramelized Milk over the brownie batter and, dragging a knife in a back-and-forth motion, create swirls of caramel in the batter.

Bake for about 35 minutes, until the edges are firm and the center is set.

Cool completely. Cut into pieces (see Element 11, page 7).

Wrapped, the brownies will keep for about 4 days at room temperature.

peanut butter brownies

It's definitely possible that you could stir up to 1 cup of peanut butter chips or perhaps even peanut butter cups into this brownie batter. Outrageous? Yes. I am, right now, imagining that possibility—the peanut butter swirl on top with bits and pieces of peanut-buttery candy below. Please do this and then come visit. Bring the brownies. Thank you.

solid gold

Baking Gold Mix makes brownie making so simple that you'll be wondering why you haven't been making brownies a minimum of three times a week for years. These peanut butter brownies are no different—the part that may seem complicated (swirling in the peanut butter topping) adds no difficulty to the recipe; it's merely an additional step (and perhaps another bowl to wash). If you'd like to skip the stovetop for warming the peanut butter, it can be done in your microwave. Simply warm the peanut butter until it's melty and then stir in the sugar and vanilla.

Preheat the oven to 350°F. Line a 9 by 13-inch pan with parchment paper (see Element 5, page 4).

In a medium saucepan, melt the butter over medium heat. In a medium bowl, combine the sugar and cocoa powder. Once the butter has melted, add the sugar, cocoa powder, and vanilla to the butter and stir. Keep the pan on the heat for about 2 minutes, stirring continuously. The mixture will look granulated. Remove the pan from the heat. Add the eggs, stirring until they are fully incorporated and everything looks smooth and glossy. Add the Baking Gold Mix and stir until you no longer see traces of it. The batter will be very thick.

Tip the saucepan and ease the batter into the prepared pan, spreading it to the corners.

Warm the peanut butter in a small saucepan. Once it's melty, stir in the powdered sugar. The mixture will be thick.

¾ cup / 170g unsalted butter, at cool room temperature (see page 151)

2 cups / 400g granulated sugar

1 cup / 100g cocoa powder

1 Tbsp / 18g pure vanilla extract

3 large eggs, cracked into a bowl and stirred with a fork

1 cup / 120g Baking Gold Mix (page 146)

1 cup / 270g smooth peanut butter

¼ cup / 29g powdered sugar

Yield: 12 large or 24 small brownies

continued →

peanut butter brownies, continued

Plop dollops of the peanut butter over the top of the brownie batter, then use a knife to work it into the batter by dragging the knife tip back and forth through the entire surface of the batter.

Bake for about 35 minutes, until the edges are firm and the center is set.

Cool completely. Cut into pieces (see Element 11, page 7).

Wrapped, the brownies will keep at room temperature for about 4 days.

Appendices

Sharing Gold

While I do love eating all the cinnamon rolls, cakes, buttercreams, cookies, and brownies in *Baking Gold*, what I really love is sharing what I've baked with others. I always say that the secret ingredient in all of my baking is my whole heart, and I mean it. I want people to know how I feel about them, and one of my favorite ways to do that is by showering them with superior sweets.

Wrapping up a package of cookies for a friend makes me happy, and inviting people over for a brownie or sprinkle party fills me with giddy anticipation for days in advance. It's all fun, thoughtful, unexpected, and full of love—exactly how I like to live.

I have a few ideas for sharing sweets and experiences in fun and unexpected ways. I hope they inspire you to create your own unique experiences for the people you love. There's nothing like dazzling your friends and family with treats.

Best Brownie Party

Welcome to the Best Brownie Party, ever! You've never been to a brownie party, you say? The time has come to change that, and I'm more than happy to help lead the way. Brownie parties involve many brownies and lots of additional ingredients that allow your guests to make any kind of brownies they'd like. Customization makes people feel extra-special, and this party is all about customization.

Perfect for: Sleepovers, birthday parties, school holidays, Galentine's Day celebrations, and television marathons.

You'll need:

A group of friends

Brownie batter

Mix-ins and toppings

Parchment paper, twine, and anything else you like for packaging

The first step is to invite your friends over. It doesn't matter how many—in my opinion, even two people make a party.

Prepare some brownie batter (see pages 173–184). I like to make enough batter for four pans of brownies—that way you can get extra creative with your brownie design and creation. The key is to make four separate batches of brownie batter so you can make four different types of brownies. Wait, didn't I say a party can be made up of two people? And then I said to make four pans of brownies? I did. Please don't question it.

Now you're ready for mix-ins and toppings. Here are some ideas:

Hard candy

Candy bars

Cookies

Toffee bits

Caramel

Mini marshmallows

Chocolate

Nut butter

Dried fruit

Nuts

Sprinkles

Potato chips

Pretzels

Gather your guests around a workspace that you've set with brownie batter, bowls of mix-ins, baking pans, and spoons. Invite your guests to design the brownies of their dreams with any of the mix-ins you've got, about 2 cups per batch. The magic happens when your guests get to do what they want with the brownies, and if more than 2 cups of extra stuff is what someone wants to do, who am I (or you) to stop it? Mix-ins can be stirred into the batter or pressed on top of the batter once it's in the pan—or both. It's entirely up to you.

After everyone has had their fun and the brownie batter is packed with odds and ends of this and that, it's time to bake.

Spread the batter into parchment paper–lined 9 by 13-inch pans. The batter will be very thick, so it will need some coaxing with a spoon or spatula to get it into the corners of the pan. If you've saved any mix-ins for the top of the brownies, add them now.

Bake at 350°F for 30–35 minutes, depending upon the amount of stuff you mixed in (more mix-ins may mean you need to add 10 or so minutes to the baking time).

Once the brownies have cooled a little, they're ready to enjoy. Now's the time to grab a gallon of milk or (I dare say) a carton of vanilla ice cream.

When the brownies are completely cool, any leftovers can be wrapped up so your guests can take them home. Waxed paper bags or sheets of parchment make easy wraps for brownies (and bars). Kitchen twine is great for securing wrapped brownies.

To: Sara
♡ Jami

Cookie Dough Drop-Off

I am especially skilled in the art of the cookie dough drop-off. I'm not saying that I alone invented this concept, yet I will tell you that the reaction you get from your friends after you treat them to a surprise bundle of ready-to-bake cookie dough will make you feel like you're the only person on earth who has ever thought to do such a thing—and it's a wonderful feeling.

Perfect for: Surprising someone you love, thank-you gifts, massive apologies, and everything in between.

You'll need:

Cookie dough packaging materials: Parchment paper or other wrapping of your choice and twine or ribbon

Freshly made and scooped cookie dough, refrigerated until firm (see pages 149–161 and 164–170)

Card stock, index card, or recipe card

On a piece of parchment paper, line up the scoops of refrigerated dough on their sides. Roll the paper around them to form a tube, leaving enough paper on each end to tie the tube with twine or ribbon to close.

Use the card stock or index card to write out some simple baking instructions for the recipient. It might be nice to remind them to freeze the dough if they don't plan on baking the cookies right away. It's also smart to include details on how long the cookies will last after baking (all of this information can be found in the cookie recipe you're using). I like to include a few pieces of parchment paper, cut to sheet-pan size and rolled up like a scroll, and I indicate on the baking instructions card what the parchment is for (to line baking pans, of course!). If you can find a glass bottle of milk at your local grocery (and can keep it cold), that'd be the sweetest finishing touch. The cold cookie dough, baking instructions, parchment paper, and milk can be bundled together in a simple tote or basket. I like to leave my cookie surprise on my friends' porches—then I ring the doorbell and skedaddle!

Cookie Party

Christmas is, of course, the ultimate reason for a cookie party, although I've been known to throw cookie parties for other holidays, including Valentine's Day, Easter, and that year we had eleven snow days in a row and our neighborhood kids couldn't take the boredom anymore. This is the kind of party that everyone loves. Make some hot chocolate, turn on some music, set the table with bowls of sprinkles and buttercream. Add in a stack of spreaders and a tray of themed cut-out cookies that have been baked (and cooled) and you're ready to cookie-party!

Perfect for: Holiday parties, Santa's cookie plate, gift giving, and snow days.

You'll need:

A group of friends

A selection of pre-baked Cut-Out Cookies (see page 63)

2 recipes Vanilla Buttercream (page 50)

Sprinkles (see Sprinkle Party, page 200)

Spatulas or butter knives for spreading

Piping bags fitted with plain tips (optional)

Cookie packaging materials: Small boxes, decorative bags, parchment, and twine or ribbon

First, create a workspace for each cookie party participant by setting out a sheet of parchment paper and placing cookies, buttercream, sprinkles, and spreaders within reach. With all the supplies right there, you can start creating: Using the parchment paper as a decorating placemat, spread or pipe the buttercream onto the tops of the cookies, then decorate them with sprinkles. Share ideas and get creative! Smaller cookies can be turned into cookie sandwiches with buttercream in the middle, sprinkles can be mixed up to create new color combinations, and you can even give the buttercream a little pizzazz by squeezing in a drop or two of color.

Once all the cookies are adorned with buttercream and sprinkles, they're ready to pack up (so your guests can take them home). Parchment paper can make a nice little bundle of cookies. Place the decorated cookies in the center of the parchment, then fold the sides in on the cookies. Secure with ribbon or twine. Alternatively, arrange the decorated cookies on a paper plate and wrap the plate in parchment. Secure the parchment with twine or tape.

Sprinkle Party

Oh wow, do I love a sprinkle party. Or a party with sprinkles. Or a party because of sprinkles. Sprinkles in general are such a happy invention, aren't they? For this sprinkle party you'll gather a few friends and some dyeable sprinkles. Crystal sugar, tiny white nonpareils, and even white jimmies can be dyed any color you'd like. Sprinkle parties are a good time to prepare for an upcoming event that will need sprinkles. Think Christmas, birthday parties, spring holidays. Custom-made, hand-dyed sprinkles make really fun gifts, especially when they are all jazzed up in cute jars.

Perfect for: Christmas cookie preparations, birthday parties, class projects, and gift giving.

You'll need:

A group of friends

8–12 cups sprinkles, depending upon how many cups of sprinkles you'd like to color

4–6 shades gel food coloring

Food-safe gloves

Parchment paper

Sprinkle packaging: Small jars with lids or cellophane bags with ties

To begin, prepare the spot where your sprinkles will dry. A wedge of spare countertop space is perfect for this—you'll pour each shade of your newly dyed sprinkles onto individual sheets of parchment, then nestle those parchment sheets together so that the sprinkles are separated yet you aren't taking up a ton of space. Overlapping parchment is okay and will not prevent your sprinkles from drying.

Using about a cup of sprinkles at a time, pour them into a bowl and add a few drops of coloring. To expand your color palette from 4–6 hues to even more, mix a few drops of 1 color with a drop of another. Yellow and blue make green, of course. And blue and red make purple. Pink and blue make lavender. One drop of yellow added to 5 drops of blue will make teal. You can create an entire rainbow of sprinkle colors with a few bottles of gel food coloring. Wearing food-safe gloves, rub the color into the sprinkles until they are a uniform color. (When changing colors, I rinse my glove while it's on my hand then dry it with a paper towel. I use fewer gloves that way.) Spread the sprinkles on a sheet of parchment and set aside to dry.

You can expand your sprinkle collection even further by creating your own signature sprinkle color mixes. Pink and purple, aqua and yellow, orange and hot pink—with your custom colors plus a selection of sprinkle mixes, you'll have the coolest sprinkle pantry in town (and so will your party guests!).

Giving Gold

Baking Gold is bursting with delights that are meant to be shared. Dotted throughout these pages are recipes for sauces, mixes, and mix-ins that can be wrapped up and given as the sweetest of gifts. These ideas are perfect for party favors, letter carrier surprises, babysitter bonuses, and hostess/host gifts.

I like to start giving gold by taking stock of what I have available for packaging. I'm a self-confessed jam jar hoarder—I seem to have a limitless supply tucked away in my kitchen cabinets, and I use them up by filling them with all the things I want to give. A jam jar filled with something like Cinnamon-Sugar Dust, a tag explaining how to use it, and a short length of twine are all you need to start giving gold.

Ideas for Giving

Baking Gold Mix (page 146): Pick a cookie recipe from *Baking Gold* that you'd like to share. Copy the recipe onto a recipe card. Scoop the amount of Baking Gold Mix called for in the recipe into a jar and attach a label so the recipient knows what's inside. Tie the recipe card to the jar with a bit of twine or ribbon.

Cinnamon-Sugar Dust (page 25): Whip up some dust, spoon it into jars, and dream up a fancy label. Include some tips on how to use the dust—even cinnamon toast will be more delicious with this special stuff.

Hot Fudge Sauce: The Cocoa Fudge Sauce (page 103) moonlights as hot fudge. Pour it into jars, and label with instructions on how to store, reheat, and use. Think ice cream sundaes, cookie dip, and even a cake glaze.

Custom Sprinkle Mix: Create a signature sprinkle mix (see facing page) and share it with anyone you can! Sprinkles accompanied by a few birthday candles would make the sweetest birthday surprise.

Decorate Your Own: Surprise someone special with an Everyday Holiday Cookie baking kit. Include a cylinder of Butter Dough (page 46), a tub of buttercream (page 50), and a jar of custom sprinkles (see facing page). They'll bake and decorate (and will be so thankful for such a thoughtful surprise). Don't forget to include a card with baking instructions.

Chocolate-Honey-Almond Butter (page 33): Ahh, a jar of this stuff makes a fantastic gift, especially when paired with bread for toasting. Include a tag with tips on rewarming the refrigerated butter.

Materials and Resources

The materials and resources used in *Baking Gold* are all easy to find and ultimately useful in a baking kitchen. For tips on storing pans and on arranging baking tools in an easy-to-access spot, Element 6 on page 5.

Baking Gold Pans

You can buy sheet pans, standard muffin pans, and 9 by 13-inch pans (with sharp corners and straight sides!) at any kitchen supply store or online. There are many metal pan makers out there. I prefer pans made by USA Pan.

Batter Bowl

I'll admit I do have a dedicated batter bowl for mixing cakes. It's a wide bowl with low sides. The low sides make it easier to stir what's inside. If you're on the lookout for a new batter bowl, a wide, low bowl will be a welcome addition to your kitchen.

Bowl Scraper

In most recipes I ask that you scrape the bottom and the sides of your bowl. The most useful tool for this is a bowl scraper, although a silicone spatula will work, too. I like bowl scrapers because I can hold the scraper itself in my hand (instead of the stick handle that's attached to a silicone spatula). With my hand on the bowl scraper I can really control what's happening with my dough or batter.

Canned and Frozen Fruit

For canned dark sweet cherries, pitted in syrup, I prefer the Oregon Specialty Fruit brand. Their website lists stores and online retailers that sell their product. These cherries are not hard to find.

For frozen berries, use any good-quality frozen berries you like—and if you pick your own in the summertime, don't forget to freeze some for future use.

Cocoa Powder

If you peel back a layer of the ins and outs of cocoa powder, you'll find that there are two main types: Dutch process and natural. I use whatever cocoa powder I have in my pantry. I invite you to investigate further or stick with me and use what you've got.

Crystal or Sparkling Sugar

I love crystal sugar because you can color it and use it for sprinkles. Some people call it crystal sugar, some people call it sparkling sugar—it comes clear and it looks like sprinkles (not a fine dust like regular granulated sugar). Bob's Red Mill packages and sells it as Sparkling Sugar. C&H calls it Pure Cane Colored Crystals. You can find it online and at some kitchen supply stores.

Gel Food Coloring

I prefer gel to traditional food coloring because it produces a more vibrant color, yet you only need a tiny bit. I like gel for coloring sprinkles (and buttercream, if you like that sort of thing).

Gel food coloring (sometimes called gel paste) can be purchased online and in the cake decorating section of crafts stores and kitchen supply stores.

Instant Yeast

I like a brand of instant yeast called Saf-Instant (in the red bag) made by Lesaffre Yeast Corporation. I purchase it through King Arthur Flour's website, although it's widely available online. You'll find all sorts of other things to order from King Arthur when you're there (I love the Vietnamese cinnamon they sell!).

Nuts, Dried Fruits, and Mix-ins

If you've never shopped at nuts.com, I'm sorry to tell you about it. When I discovered nuts.com I nearly fainted and then almost spent all of my money. Every kind of nut, dried fruit, ribbon candy, hard candy, or gummy candy you could ever want can be found on nuts.com. They even carry sprinkles and chocolate nonpareil candies in both white and rainbow (tailor-made for the Fun Time Surprise Cake on page 132).

Parchment Paper

You can buy parchment in boxes of 1,000 sheets. Look for sheets that are 16 by 24 inches. I like these oversized sheets because they can be used as is, or they can be cut to fit sheet pans and muffin pans.

I buy mine at a food-service supply store in the paper goods aisle. A 1,000-sheet box will last for a very long time, and, yes!—you will find tons of uses for parchment.

Peanut Butter

I do like to bake with natural peanut butter (containing only peanuts and salt), yet I've found that baking with any old peanut butter works. I like JIF Natural as an economical, easy-to-find option, yet you can use any peanut butter you like in *Baking Gold* recipes.

Pearl Sugar

If you're placing an order at King Arthur Flour, add some pearl sugar to your list. Otherwise you can probably find it in the baking section of a well-stocked grocery store or on Amazon.

Scale

I like the predictability that baking by weight provides, and while I'm not insisting you buy a scale, I am telling you you'll have more success if you bake by weight instead of by volume. The true amount of all-purpose flour in 1 cup will never be exact and will always vary from cup to cup. Compare that to the 120 grams that 1 cup of all-purpose flour weighs, and there's no contest because 120 grams of all-purpose flour will always be 120 grams. This precision (and the desire for it) is pure Baking Gold. My favorite kitchen scales are made by My Weigh.

Scoops

If you don't have a trusty 2 Tbsp / 30ml scoop, treat yourself and pick one up. Buy one from King Arthur Flour or get one at the same food service store where you buy your box of parchment paper.

Sifter

For smooth buttercream, powdered sugar should always be sifted. You can use any fine-mesh strainer—simply dump in the sugar and push it through the mesh. Alternatively, you can get a sifter called a *tamis*. A tamis can rest inside a mixing bowl and the bowl can be placed on your scale. Zero out the scale, then scoop the sugar directly into the tamis until you reach the weight specified in the recipe—then sift away. Tamises are widely available in kitchen supply stores and online.

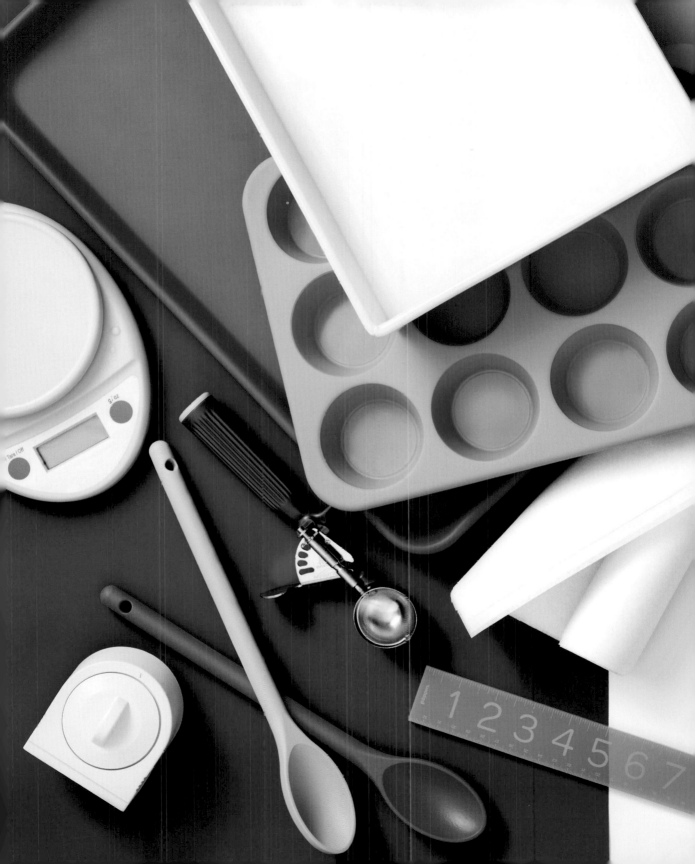

Stand Mixer

A stand mixer can be something you save up for, something you put on your wish list, or something you find for a total steal by scouring the internet and happening upon a closeout color or (if you time it right) the exact color and model you're looking for that's been refurbished by KitchenAid. I like a 6- or 7-quart model, though a 5-quart mixer is perfect for mixing up Baking Gold recipes.

White Nonpareils

You know these sprinkles—they're the tiny white balls that come on everything from cookies to cake. You can find them in the baking section of your grocery store or online at nuts.com.

acknowledgments

A gigantic, golden thank-you to:

Alison Fargis and Jenny Wapner

Caitlin Haught Brown and Andrea Greco

Maggie Kirkland

Annie Marino, Lorena Jones, Emma Campion, Jane Chinn and the rest of the team at Ten Speed Press

Jessica Palace and Todd Henry

Emily Kate Roemer and Alea Zielinski

Sara Stovall and Stephanie Sheldon-Nevarez

Theo James Spiesman Curl, Ken Norris, Birdie, Bruce Chips, and Louie Domino

index

a

almond butter
    Chocolate–Honey–Almond Butter, 33
    Chocolate–Honey–Almond Butter
        Poufs, 33–34
almonds
    Apple-Cherry Crisp with
        Almonds, 84
    Raspberry Jam and Almond
        Tarts, 45
    Sweet Cherry Crumble Bars, 68–70
    toasting, 21
apples
    Apple, Butter, and Brown Sugar
        Tarts, 45
    Apple-Cherry Crisp with
        Almonds, 84
    Apple-Citrus Crisp, 83–84
    Apple-Vanilla Crisp, 83
    Spiced Apple Crisp, 84
apricots
    Apricot-Walnut Caramel, 87
    Apricot-Walnut Caramel Tarts with
        Honey Cream, 87–88

b

Baking Gold Mix, 146
bars
    Blueberry-Coconut-Orange
        Ones, 77
    Butterscotch, Cashew, Coconut
        Goodie Snacktime Bars, 79
    Chocolate, Peanut, Sea Salt Goodie
        Snacktime Bars, 83
    Goodie Snacktime Bars, 78–79
    Jam Jambles, 66–67
    Maple-Pecan Not-Pie Bars, 71–73
    Nutty Chocolate Oaties, 80–81
    pans for, 7
    Peanut Butter and Jam Jambles, 67
    Peanut Butter, Raisin, Cinnamon
        Goodie Snacktime Bars, 79
    size of, 7
    Sweet Cherry Crumble Bars, 68–70

batter bowls, 205
batters
    Chocolate–Sour Cream Batter,
        96–97
    Vanilla–Sour Cream Batter, 118–20
berries
    Berry-Cardamom Cookies with
        Toasted Walnuts, 159–61
    frozen, 205
    See also individual berries
Bits of Chocolate and Sea Salt Cookies,
    149–51
Blackberry Crisp, Peach-, 84
blueberries
    Berry-Cardamom Cookies with
        Toasted Walnuts, 159–61
    Blueberry-Coconut-Orange Ones, 77
    Blueberry-Coconut-Orange Topping,
        77
    Blueberry Crumble Cake with Citrus–
        Vanilla Cream Glaze, 130
    Blueberry-Orange Cake with Vanilla
        Bean Cream Cheese Buttercream,
        130
    Citrus–Vanilla Cream–Glazed
        Blueberry Cake, 129–30
    Nectarine and Blueberry Tarts, 45
bowl scrapers, 205
brownies
    Best Brownie Party, 190
    Caramelized Milk Brownies, 178–80
    Double Vanilla–Spice Brownies, 177
    Fruit and Nut Brownies, 173–74
    Malted Milk–White Chocolate
        Brownies, 171
    pans for, 7
    Peanut Butter Brownies, 182–84
    removing parchment paper
        from, 174
    size of, 7
brown sugar, 5
    Brown Sugar–Cardamom Butter
        Stack-Ups, 37–38
    Brown Sugar–Oat Dough, 74
Bubble Bun Dust, 29

buns
    Caramel Sticky Buns, 21–22
    Coconut Sticky Buns, 22
    pans for, 7
    Spiced Bubble Buns, 29–30
butter, 5
    Butter Dough, 46–48
    Cardamom-Ginger Butter, 37
buttercream
    amount of, for topping cakes, 97
    Cherry Cream Buttercream, 111–12
    Cream Cheese Buttercream, 99–100
    Peanut Butter Buttercream, 103–4
    Peppermint Buttercream, 107–8
    Special Chocolate Buttercream, 123
    Vanilla Buttercream, 50–52
butterscotch
    Butterscotch, Cashew, Coconut
        Goodie Snacktime Bars, 79
    Butterscotch Whipped Cream, 137
    Peach and Butterscotch Whipped
        Cream Cake, 138
    Strawberry and Butterscotch
        Whipped Cream Cake, 137–38

c

cakes
    baking time for, 97
    Blueberry Crumble Cake with Citrus–
        Vanilla Cream Glaze, 130
    Blueberry-Orange Cake with Vanilla
        Bean Cream Cheese Buttercream,
        130
    Chocolate-Cherry Cake, 111–12
    Chocolate-Peppermint Cake, 107–8
    Cinnamon Crumble Cake, 126
    Citrus–Vanilla Cream–Glazed
        Blueberry Cake, 129–30
    Cocoa Fudge–Glazed Peanut Butter
        Cake, 104
    Crunchy, Creamy Coconut
        Cake, 139
    Everyday Chocolate Cake, 99–100
    fancy, 120

Fun Time Surprise Cake, 132–35
Marshmallow-Cocoa Cake, 114–17
pans for, 7
Peach and Butterscotch Whipped
    Cream Cake, 138
Peanut Butter–Fudge Polka Dot
    Cake, 103–4
Strawberry and Butterscotch
    Whipped Cream Cake, 137–38
Toffee Fudge Cake, 139
Vanilla Celebration Cake, 123–24
Candy Pop Cookies, 64
caramel
    Apricot-Walnut Caramel, 87
    Caramel-Pecan Sauce, 21
    Caramel Sticky Buns, 21–22
cardamom
    Brown Sugar–Cardamom Butter
        Stack-Ups, 37–38
    Cardamom-Ginger Butter, 37
    Cardamom-Raisin Stack-Ups, 38
Cashew, Butterscotch, Coconut Goodie
    Snacktime Bars, 79
cheese
    Aged Cheddar and Pear Tarts, 45
    Cheese-and-Herb Stack-Ups, 38
    Cream Cheese Buttercream, 99–100
    Crispy Kale, Parmesan, and Egg
        Tarts, 45
    Goat Cheese and Pesto
        Tarts, 45
    Gruyère and Caramelized Onion
        Tarts, 45
    Smoked Mozzarella and Tomato
        Tarts, 45
cherries
    Apple-Cherry Crisp with
        Almonds, 84
    canned, 205
    Cherry Cream Buttercream, 111–12
    Chocolate-Cherry Cake, 111–12
    Fruit and Nut Brownies, 173–74
    Goodie Snacktime Bars, 78–79
    Pretzel-Toffee-Chocolate-Cherry
        Cookies, 153–54
    Sweet Cherry Compote, 68
    Sweet Cherry Crumble Bars, 68–70
chocolate, 5, 8
    Bits of Chocolate and Sea Salt
        Cookies, 149–51
    Caramelized Milk Brownies, 178–80
    Chocolate and Hazelnut Tarts, 45

Chocolate Buttercream Darlings, 60
Chocolate-Cherry Cake, 111–12
Chocolate-Chocolate-Chocolate
    Cookies, 169–70
Chocolate-Chocolate–Peanut
    Butter Cookies, 170
Chocolate-Honey–Almond
    Butter, 33
Chocolate-Honey–Almond Butter
    Poufs, 33–34
Chocolate, Peanut, Sea Salt Goodie
    Snacktime Bars, 83
Chocolate-Pecan-Toffee
    Cookies, 151
Chocolate-Peppermint Cake, 107–8
Chocolate Poufs, 34
Chocolate–Sour Cream Batter,
    96–97
Cocoa Fudge–Glazed Peanut Butter
    Cake, 104
Cocoa Fudge Sauce, 103–4
cocoa powder, 205
Double Vanilla–Spice Brownies, 177
Everyday Chocolate Cake, 99–100
Fruit and Nut Brownies, 173–74
Fun Time Surprise Cake, 132–35
Malted Milk–White Chocolate
    Brownies, 171
Marshmallow-Cocoa Cake, 114–17
Nutty Chocolate Oaties, 80–81
Peanut Butter Brownies, 182–84
Peanut Butter–Chocolate Cookies,
    164–67
Peanut Butter–Fudge Polka Dot
    Cake, 103–4
Pretzel-Toffee-Chocolate-Cherry
    Cookies, 153–54
Special Chocolate Buttercream, 123
Toffee-Chocolate Cookies, 154
Toffee Fudge Cake, 139
See also white chocolate
cinnamon, 26
    Cinnamon Crumb Cake, 126
    Cinnamon-Sugar Darlings, 60
    Cinnamon-Sugar Dust, 25
    Gooey Cinnamon Swirls, 25–26
citrus
    Citrus–Vanilla Cream Dots, 55
    Citrus–Vanilla Cream Glaze, 129
    Citrus–Vanilla Cream–Glazed
        Blueberry Cake, 129–30
    See also individual fruits

cocoa powder. See chocolate
coconut
    Blueberry-Coconut-Orange
        Ones, 77
    Blueberry-Coconut-Orange Topping,
        77
    Butterscotch, Cashew, Coconut
        Goodie Snacktime Bars, 79
    Caramelized Milk and Coconut
        Tarts, 45
    Coconut Jam Tarts, 41–42
    Coconut Sticky Buns, 22
    Crunchy, Creamy Coconut
        Cake, 139
    Nutty Chocolate Oaties, 80–81
    toasting, 22
compotes
    Strawberry Compote, 66
    Sweet Cherry Compote, 68
cookies
    Berry-Cardamom Cookies with
        Toasted Walnuts, 159–61
    Bits of Chocolate and Sea Salt
        Cookies, 149–51
    Candy Pop Cookies, 64
    Chocolate Buttercream
        Darlings, 60
    Chocolate-Chocolate-Chocolate
        Cookies, 169–70
    Chocolate-Chocolate–Peanut
        Butter Cookies, 170
    Chocolate-Pecan-Toffee
        Cookies, 151
    Cinnamon-Sugar Darlings, 60
    Citrus–Vanilla Cream Dots, 55
    Cookie Dough Drop-Off, 195
    Cookie Party, 196
    Cut-Out Cookies with Buttercream
        and Sprinkles, 52
    Darling Buttercream Darlings, 58–60
    Everyday Holiday Cookies, 50–52
    Ginger-Molasses Cookies with
        Orange Zest, 157–58
    Lemon Zest Darlings, 60
    pans for, 7, 151
    Peanut Butter–Chocolate Cookies,
        164–67
    Peanut Butter Cookies, 167
    Pretzel-Toffee-Chocolate-Cherry
        Cookies, 153–54
    Sprinkle Pop Cookies, 63–64
    Toffee-Chocolate Cookies, 154

Cream Cheese Buttercream, 99–100
crisps
    Apple-Cherry Crisp with Almonds, 84
    Apple-Citrus Crisp, 83–84
    Apple-Vanilla Crisp, 83
    Peach-Blackberry Crisp, 84
    Spiced Apple Crisp, 84
crystal sugar, 205
Cut-Out Cookies with Buttercream and
    Sprinkles, 52

d

Darling Buttercream Darlings, 58–60
Double Vanilla–Spice Brownies, 177
doughs
    Brown Sugar–Oat Dough, 74
    Butter Dough, 46–48
    Overnight Dough, 16–18
dusts
    Bubble Bun Dust, 29
    Cinnamon-Sugar Dust, 25

e

Egg Tarts, Crispy Kale, Parmesan, and, 45

f

food coloring, 205
freezing, 5
fruits
    canned and frozen, 205
    Fruit and Nut Brownies, 173–74
    substituting, 8
    See also individual fruits
Fun Time Surprise Cake, 132–35

g

gift ideas, 195, 201
ginger
    Cardamom-Ginger Butter, 37
    Ginger-Molasses Cookies with
        Orange Zest, 157–58
glazes
    Citrus–Vanilla Cream Glaze, 129
    Marshmallow Glaze, 114
Goodie Snacktime Bars, 78–79
Gooey Cinnamon Swirls, 25–26

h

Hazelnut Tarts, Chocolate and, 45
Honey Cream, 87–88

j

jam
    Coconut Jam Tarts, 41–42
    Jam Jambles, 66–67
    Peanut Butter and Jam Jambles, 67
    Raspberry Jam and Almond Tarts, 45

k

Kale, Parmesan, and Egg Tarts, Crispy,
    45

l

labeling, importance of, 4, 5
Lemon Zest Darlings, 60

m

Malted Milk–White Chocolate Brownies,
    171
maple syrup
    Maple-Pecan Filling, 71
    Maple-Pecan Not-Pie Bars, 71–73
marshmallows
    Marshmallow-Cocoa Cake, 114–17
    Marshmallow Glaze, 114
measuring cups and spoons, 4
Milk, Caramelized, 178
    Caramelized Milk and Coconut Tarts,
        45
    Caramelized Milk Brownies, 178–80
mixers, 4, 208

n

Nectarine and Blueberry Tarts, 45
nuts
    Fruit and Nut Brownies, 173–74
    Nutty Chocolate Oaties, 80–81
    sources of, 206
    substituting, 8
    toasting, 21
    See also individual nuts

o

oats, 74
    Brown Sugar–Oat Dough, 74
    Nutty Chocolate Oaties, 80–81
Onion, Caramelized, and Gruyère Tarts, 45
oranges
    Blueberry-Coconut-Orange Ones, 77
    Blueberry-Coconut-Orange Topping,
        77
    Blueberry-Orange Cake with Vanilla
        Bean Cream Cheese Buttercream,
        130
    Ginger-Molasses Cookies with
        Orange Zest, 157–58
oven thermometers, 4
Overnight Dough, 16–18

p

pans, 4, 7, 205
parchment paper, 4, 174, 206
parties
    Best Brownie Party, 190
    Cookie Party, 196
    Sprinkle Party, 200
peaches
    Peach and Butterscotch Whipped
        Cream Cake, 138
    Peach-Blackberry Crisp, 84
Peanut, Chocolate, and Sea Salt Goodie
    Snacktime Bars, 83
peanut butter, 206
    Chocolate-Chocolate–Peanut Butter
        Cookies, 170
    Cocoa Fudge–Glazed Peanut Butter
        Cake, 104
    Peanut Butter and Jam Jambles, 67
    Peanut Butter Brownies, 182–84
    Peanut Butter Buttercream, 103–4
    Peanut Butter–Chocolate Cookies,
        164–67
    Peanut Butter Cookies, 167
    Peanut Butter–Fudge Polka Dot Cake,
        103–4
    Peanut Butter, Raisin, Cinnamon
        Goodie Snacktime Bars, 79
pearl sugar, 206
Pear Tarts, Aged Cheddar and, 45
pecans
    Caramel-Pecan Sauce, 21
    Caramel Sticky Buns, 21–22

Chocolate-Pecan-Toffee Cookies, 151
Fruit and Nut Brownies, 173–74
Maple-Pecan Filling, 71
Maple-Pecan Not-Pie Bars, 71–73
toasting, 21
Peppermint Buttercream, 107–8
poufs
    Chocolate-Honey–Almond Butter
        Poufs, 33–34
    Chocolate Poufs, 34
Pretzel-Toffee-Chocolate-Cherry
    Cookies, 153–54

r

raisins
    Cardamom-Raisin Stack-Ups, 38
    Fruit and Nut Brownies, 173–74
    Peanut Butter, Raisin, Cinnamon
        Goodie Snacktime Bars, 79
Raspberry Jam and Almond Tarts, 45
recipes
    choosing, 2
    making notes on, 2
    reading, 2
    reinventing, 7

s

sauces
    Caramel-Pecan Sauce, 21
    Cocoa Fudge Sauce, 103–4
scales, 4, 206
scoops, 7, 154, 206
sifters, 206
sparkling sugar, 205
sprinkles
    nonpareils, white, 208
    Sprinkle Party, 200
    Sprinkle Pop Cookies, 63–64
stack-ups
    Brown Sugar–Cardamom Butter
        Stack-Ups, 37–38
    Cardamom-Raisin Stack-Ups, 38
    Cheese-and-Herb Stack-Ups, 38
strawberries
    Strawberry and Butterscotch
        Whipped Cream Cake, 137–38
    Strawberry Compote, 66
substitutions, 5, 7, 8
sugars, 8, 205, 206

t

tarts
    Aged Cheddar and Pear Tarts, 45
    Apple, Butter, and Brown Sugar
        Tarts, 45
    Apricot-Walnut Caramel Tarts with
        Honey Cream, 87–88
    Caramelized Milk and Coconut
        Tarts, 45
    Chocolate and Hazelnut Tarts, 45
    Coconut Jam Tarts, 41–42
    Crispy Kale, Parmesan, and Egg
        Tarts, 45
    Goat Cheese and Pesto Tarts, 45
    Gruyère and Caramelized Onion
        Tarts, 45
    Nectarine and Blueberry Tarts, 45
    pans for, 7
    Raspberry Jam and Almond
        Tarts, 45
    Smoked Mozzarella and Tomato
        Tarts, 45
    steps for, 42
toffee, 79
    Chocolate-Pecan-Toffee
        Cookies, 151
    Crunchy, Creamy Coconut
        Cake, 139
    Fruit and Nut Brownies, 173–74
    Goodie Snacktime Bars, 78–79
    Pretzel-Toffee-Chocolate-Cherry
        Cookies, 153–54
    Toffee-Chocolate Cookies, 154
    Toffee Fudge Cake, 139
Tomato Tarts, Smoked Mozzarella
    and, 45

v

vanilla, 5
    Double Vanilla–Spice Brownies, 177
    Vanilla Buttercream, 50–52
    Vanilla Celebration Cake, 123–24
    Vanilla–Sour Cream Batter, 118–20

w

walnuts
    Apricot-Walnut Caramel, 87
    Apricot-Walnut Caramel Tarts with
        Honey Cream, 87–88

Berry-Cardamom Cookies with
    Toasted Walnuts, 159–61
toasting, 21
Whipped Cream, Butterscotch, 137
white chocolate
    Chocolate-Chocolate-Chocolate
        Cookies, 169–70
    Goodie Snacktime Bars, 78–79
    Malted Milk–White Chocolate
        Brownies, 171

y

yeast, 206

Published in the United States by Ten Speed Press, an imprint of Random House, a division of
Penguin Random House LLC, New York.
www.tenspeed.com

Ten Speed Press and the Ten Speed Press colophon are registered trademarks of Penguin Random
House LLC.

Library of Congress Cataloging-in-Publication Data:
Names: Curl, Jami, author. | Roemer, Emily Kate, photographer.
Title: Baking gold : how to bake (almost) everything with 3 doughs, 2 batters, and 1 magic mix /
Jami Curl ; photographs by Emily Kate Roemer.
Description: First edition. | Emeryville : Ten Speed Press, 2019. | Includes bibliographical references
    and index.
Identifiers: LCCN 2019029977 | ISBN 9781984856654 (hardback) | ISBN 9781984856661 (epub)
Subjects: LCSH: Baking. | Pastry. | Desserts.
Classification: LCC TX763 .C87 2019 | DDC 641.81/5--dc23
LC record available at https://lccn.loc.gov/2019029977

Hardcover ISBN: 978-1-9848-5665-4
eBook ISBN: 978-1-9848-5665-1

Printed in China

Design by Annie Marino
Food styling by Caitlin Haught Brown
Prop styling by Andrea Greco

10 9 8 7 6 5 4 3 2 1

First Edition

3 doughs

brown sugar-oat dough
- blueberry-coconut-orange ones
- goodie snacktime bars
- nutty chocolate oaties
- apple-citrus crisp
- apricot-walnut caramel tarts with honey cream

overnight dough
- caramel sticky buns
- gooey cinnamon swirls
- spiced bubble buns
- chocolate-honey-almond butter poufs
- brown sugar-cardamom butter stack-ups
- coconut jam tarts

butter dough
- everyday holiday cookies
- citrus-vanilla cream dots
- darling buttercream darlings
- sprinkle pop cookies
- jam jambles
- sweet cherry crumble bars
- maple-pecan not-pie bars

Jami Curl is a pastry chef, home baker, and author of *Candy Is Magic*, winner of the International Association of Culinary Professionals' cookbook award for baking. Curl was named one of *Fast Company*'s 100 most creative people in food, and her work has been featured in *Food & Wine*, *Good Housekeeping*, *Real Simple*, *Martha Stewart*, *O: The Oprah Magazine*, the *Wall Street Journal*, and the *New York Times*, among other publications. She lives and bakes in Portland, Oregon.